MW00720734

UK unemployment

Third edition

Andrew Clark
OECD, Paris

Richard Layard
London School of Economics

and

Marcus Rubin
Communication Workers Union

Series Editor
Bryan Hurl
Harrow School

Dedicated to the memory of David Hattersley (1951–1996)

Heinemann Educational Publishers
Halley Court, Jordan Hill, Oxford OX2 8EJ
a division of Reed Educational & Professional Publishing Ltd

OXFORD FLORENCE PRAGUE MADRID ATHENS
MELBOURNE AUCKLAND KUALA LUMPUR SINGAPORE TOKYO
IBADAN NAIROBI KAMPALA JOHANNESBURG GABORONE
PORTSMOUTH NH (USA) CHICAGO MEXICO CITY SÃO PAULO

First published 1989
Third edition published 1997

01 00 99 98 97
10 9 8 7 6 5 4 3 2 1

British Library Cataloguing in Publication Data
A catalogue record for this book is available from the British Library

ISBN 0 435 33038 1

Typeset and illustrated by TechType, Abingdon, Oxon.
Printed and bound in Great Britain by Biddles Ltd, Guildford

Acknowledgements

The authors wish to thank the infallible Sue Kirkbride for yet another typing feat, and acknowledge the forebearance of Sue Walton and Bryan Hurl.

The Publishers would like to thank the following for permission to reproduce copyright material:

The Associated Examining Board for the questions on pp. 25, 37, 49 and 61; John Banham for the article on p. 77; S. and C. Calman for the cartoons by Mel Calman on pp. 37, 44 and 83 © S. and C. Calman; The *Economist* for the articles on p. 20, 11/12/93, on p. 38–9, 28/9/91, on p. 46, 12/10/96, on p. 57, 21/12/96, on p. 68, 8/6/96, on p. 70, 26/6/93, on p. 72, 11/2/95, and on p. 82, 20/8/94. © The *Economist*, London; HMSO for the extract from *Economic Briefing no. 7* on p. 8 and for the table from *New Earnings Survey 1993* on p. 62. Crown copyright is reproduced with the permission of the Controller of Her Majesty's Stationery Office; The *Independent* for the article on p. 5; Richard Layard for the article on p. 78; Stephen Lee for the cartoons on pp. 14 and 20; Lloyds TSB Group plc for the extract on p. 89; London Examinations. A division of Edexcel Foundation for the questions on pp. 38–9, 49–50, 61, 69 and 87–89; Northern Examinations and Assessment Board for the questions on pp. 8–9, 75, 76–8 and 87; OECD for the figures on pp. 65, 66 and 67; Office for National Statistics for the tables from *Labour Force Survey Monthly Digest of Statistics, New Earnings Survey, Social Trends* and from *Employment Gazette* on pp. 3, 6, 8–9, 11, 15, 16 and 22. Crown copyright is reproduced with the permission of the Controller of Her Majesty's Stationery Office; Philip Allan Publishers Ltd for 'The Labour Market' by John Philpott in *Focus on Britain 1994*, ed. Philip Allan, John Benyon and Barry McCormick on p. 63; Sterling Books UK for the extract from *Economics Update 1993* by G. Cook on p. 50; © Times Newspapers Ltd for the graph on p. 49, 22/2/93, the graph on p. 50, 21/2/93 and the article and graph on p. 60, 5/1/97; Reproduced by permission of the University of Cambridge Local Examinations Syndicate the questions on pp. 7, 25–26, 49, 62–3 and 87; UODLE material is reproduced by permission of the University of Cambridge Local Examinations Syndicate on pp. 38, 49, 69, 75 and 87.

The publishers have made every effort to contact the correct copyright holders. However, if any material has been incorrectly acknowledged, the publishers will be pleased to make the necessary arrangements at the earliest opportunity.

Contents

Preface

The adding of a third author has widened the level of expertise for which this volume has become noted. Seven chapters have become eight; some of their titles and contents have changed.

In this new edition, the opportunity has been taken to restructure but also integrate those aspects of other volumes in the series which are complementary to it.

UK Unemployment is an appropriate text for the Edexcel Foundation London Examinations' 9120 syllabus A2 option on labour markets and also for OCEAC's 4387 syllabus A2 option. Other relevant companion volumes are *Industrialization and deindustrialization* and *Supply side economics*.

Bryan Hurl
Series Editor

Introduction

Unemployment in the United Kingdom remains very high by historical standards. It is the major social problem of our time. Further, it contributes to other social problems such as poverty and crime. Unemployment is a waste of our national resources, a waste which can never be recovered. The goods and services the unemployed would have produced if given the chance are lost forever. In economic terms, unemployment is inefficient. So much work needs to be done, and so many people need work. Our society is clearly failing if it cannot bring these two needs together.

Further, as we shall see in Chapter 2, unemployment is also unfair. Some groups of people suffer much more unemployment than others. In the UK, as in a number of other Western countries, unemployment is concentrated on the young, the low-skilled, manual workers and males. Even those not at risk of unemployment suffer because of:

- the waste of the output that could be produced
- the taxes needed to finance unemployment benefits
- the social costs of unemployment.

Many people doubt whether anything like full employment is ever possible again. As in the 1930s, they consider unemployment as an act of God – the product of forces beyond our control. However, after the 1930s, unemployment in the 1950s and 1960s was lower than in any previous period. Our present high unemployment is quite abnormal. It could and should be much lower.

Governments do not do more to reduce unemployment because they are afraid that they will increase inflation as a result. In Chapter 3, an economic model which shows the relationship between unemployment and inflation is explained. In Chapters 4 and 5, this model is then used to help explain the performance of the UK economy, and it is shown how unemployment came to be so high. Chapter 6 then applies the model to other countries.

In Chapter 7, a few myths about unemployment are dealt with, and the last chapter outlines the debate on remedies for unemployment. Finally, we give our conclusions. We believe that the government has the power to reduce unemployment, and it should exercise this power.

Chapter One
What is unemployment?

'Complete idleness, even on an income, demoralizes.' Lord Beveridge

Definitions

What do we mean by an 'unemployed person'? Figure 1 shows standardized unemployment rates calculated by the OECD (Organisation for Economic Co-operation and Development) and based on the definition of unemployment used by the ILO (International Labour Organisation): people are counted as unemployed *if they do not have work, are actively seeking work and are in a position to start work.*

This definition of unemployment is very straightfoward. A person has to be both out of work *and* looking for work. The first part of this definition seems clear enough, because we can all see whether someone is at work or not. Yet it does not take into account a potentially important group: the 'hidden unemployed' who have only a part-time job

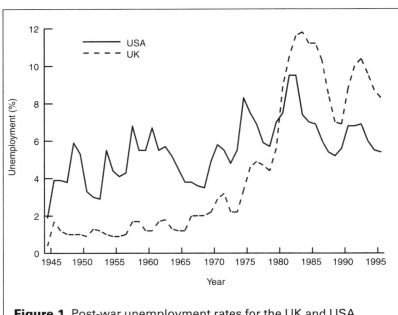

Figure 1 Post-war unemployment rates for the UK and USA

but would prefer to work full-time. And the second part of this definition is even more fuzzy, since some people seek work more intensely than others.

The concept of 'seeking work' is especially unclear for women who stopped work because they were having a child but are now keeping their eyes open in case a suitable job turns up. These women are on the boundary between **participation** and non-participation in the labour market. *Participation means taking part. The employed (including the self-employed) and the unemployed are the participants in the labour market.* Women who would like to work and who have children are classified either as non-participants or as unemployed depending on how actively they are looking for work and when they can start work. The concept of unemployment is thus clearer for males than for females, especially for males aged 25 to 50, 93 per cent of whom participate in the labour market. The non-participants, whose numbers grew in the 1980s, are mainly disabled people or students.

Female participation rates vary considerably from country to country. As a result two countries can have the same number of women of working age and the same number of unemployed women and yet have quite different female unemployment rates. This is because unemployment rates are calculated using only participants in the labour market and not the entire working age population. In international comparisons, it is therefore interesting to look separately at male unemployment. Table 1 shows the UK doing much less well for male unemployment relative to other countries than it does for overall unemployment.

Table 1 Unemployment rates by sex, 1996 (first four months)

	Males	*Females*	*All*
UK	9.8	6.5	8.4
France	9.7	13.8	11.6
Germany	8.0	10.1	8.9
Italy	9.4	17.4	12.4
Spain	17.9	29.5	22.4
Sweden	10.3	9.1	9.7
Japan	3.3	3.3	3.3
USA	5.6	5.5	5.5

The UK figures in this table come from the **Labour Force Survey.** This is a household survey of the population, carried out for the Department for Education and Employment. It gathers a wide range of information related to employment and unemployment. This allows the calculation of unemployment according to the standard international (ILO) definition described above. Other countries carry out similar surveys.

Another way of defining unemployment uses the **claimant count figures** published each month for the UK. The claimant count is simply *the number of people receiving Jobseeker's Allowance* (formerly unemployment benefit or income support). Women are much less likely than men to receive benefit. In particular, unemployed married and cohabiting women often receive no benefit. They are eligible for the Jobseeker's Allowance for six months, but only if they have paid sufficient national insurance contributions. Thus, the claimant count figure greatly understates female unemployment and does not correspond at all well to the standard international definition of unemployment. The spring 1996 Labour Force Survey showed that, of the 800 000 women unemployed according to the standard international definition, fewer than 300 000 were receiving benefit because of their unemployment.

The overall difference, however, between the claimant count figure and the international definition is not very large. While many unemployed people, particularly women, receive no benefit and are not included in the claimant count, a number of those who do receive benefit for unemployment are *not* unemployed according to the international definition. This is mainly because they do have some work, which could be for only one hour a week, or because they are not in a position to start work within two weeks, perhaps because of the need to make arrangements for the care of their children.

Another problem with the claimant count as a measure of unemployment is that it changes not only when unemployment changes but also when entitlement to benefit changes. From 1988, the government has made getting benefit for unemployment progressively more difficult. Whether or not this is a good thing, it means that the claimant count is not always a good guide to changes in unemployment.

The claimant count still has some advantages. Unlike the Labour Force Survey, it is not based on a sample of the population, but on all claimants. Thus, the claimant count is more accurate and gives more detailed information, for example on local unemployment. It also provides rapid monthly information, whereas the Labour Force Survey is quarterly. Nevertheless, a monthly Labour Force Survey might provide more credible statistics than the claimant count does (see the box).

Statistics chief says jobs count is not believed

ROSIE WATERHOUSE

The head of the Government Statistical Service has warned that the public will never regain confidence in the integrity of the official unemployment statistics unless the monthly count is changed to an internationally recognised standard.

In an interview with the *Independent,* Bill McLennan, who is also director of the Central Statistical Office, responsible for macro economic statistics and the national accounts, said that "nobody believes" the benefits claimants count.

Instead, he said, the UK should publish monthly figures from the International Labour Organisation's Labour Force Survey which defines employment and unemployment. These are published quarterly in the UK.

Lies, damn lies

"There are three kinds of lies: lies, damn lies and statistics."

Disraeli's distrust of statistics is shared by many people today. They are used – and misused – by politicians, civil servants, and officialdom in general as a tool of convenience.

Can we trust figures on issues such as crime, unemployment, inflation, spending on the NHS, hospital waiting lists, school league tables, company results? Are government statisticians sufficiently independent of political pressure?

Mr McLennan said that although the unemployment numbers were "published correctly" the public's perception was that they were not to be trusted.

"A lot more people are now willing to trust the Government's statisticians. But I'm also acutely aware that we haven't removed this problem . . . I don't think this problem will be removed until you remove the source of it. The only way we are going to stop this . . . is to spend some more money and bring out the International Labour Organisation-based definitions monthly".

The ILO definition draws in some people who are either ineligible for unemployment-related benefits or who choose not to register a claim. The claimant count takes in those with relatively low earnings from part-time work who are also claiming unemployment-related benefits legitimately. These would be classified as being employed rather than unemployed.

The Independent, 19 December 1994

The numbers game

The definition of unemployment is thus controversial. Critics of the UK government in the 1980s alleged that politicians were 'moving the goalposts' whenever they made changes that reduced entitlement to benefit and so lowered the claimant count. For example, the Social Security Act 1988 'moved the goalposts' by making almost all unemployed 16- and 17-year-olds ineligible for benefit. This reduced the claimant count by almost 100 000.

So far we have considered two ways of measuring unemployment. The Unemployment Unit has a third way. This body takes the Labour Force Survey figure, which follows the international definition, and adds the number of people who are not counted as unemployed because they have not looked for work in the four weeks before the survey. This Unemployment Unit figure, known as the 'UU Broad LFS' measure of unemployment, includes everyone who is not working, wants work and can start work within two weeks. Table 2 shows the extent to which this definition of unemployment affects the figures.

Table 2 UK unemployment figures (and percentages of labour force), spring 1996, seasonally adjusted

	Unemployment Unit 'Broad LFS'	International definition (LFS)	Claimant count
Men	1 840 000 (11.8%)	1 510 000 (9.7%)	1 620 000 (10.4%)
Women	1 370 000 (11.1%)	800 000 (6.5%)	500 000 (4.1%)
All	3 210 000 (11.5%)	2 310 000 (8.3%)	2 120 000 (7.6%)

The difference between the definitions affects more women than men. This reinforces the point made earlier about the difficulty of applying the 'seeking work' definition to women. The 'Broad LFS' definition includes women with young children who have stopped work and would like to return to work even if they have not actually sought work in the four weeks before the survey. They might, for example, be relying on friends in work to tell them of suitable vacancies. The 'Broad LFS' definition also includes **discouraged workers.** *Discouraged workers do not have work and would like to work, but are not actually looking for a job because they do not believe that they could find one if they did.* The long-term unemployed tend to become discouraged workers. One aim of government policy is to prevent this. The number of discouraged workers is counter-cyclical, falling dramatically when the economy grows rapidly and job prospects improve.

Trends in unemployment
Figure 1 on page 2 shows unemployment rates in the UK and USA since 1945. In the UK, the very low unemployment rates during the war continued through the 1940s into the 1950s and early 60s. This was the period of the UK's long-lived post-war economic boom. However, between 1965 and 1986, unemployment rose nearly every

year, peaking in 1996 at a rate only a little less than that in the Depression of the early 1930s. The average unemployment rate in the 25 years from 1942 to 1966 was 1.1 per cent. By way of contrast, the average rate in the past 25 years has been 7.4 per cent, and the average rate since 1982 has been 9.8 per cent. The two big rises in unemployment occurred between 1974 and 1976 and between 1980 and 1982 – after the first and second oil-price **shocks** respectively. *A shock describes an unforeseen event which disturbs the economic system.* Unemployment rates fell sharply from 1986 to 1990, only to rise rapidly again to double-digit levels. The fall in unemployment from 1993 onwards has been gentler, but unemployment still remains very high by historical standards. Chapters 4 and 5 consider the UK's recent unemployment experience.

The US experience contrasts with that of the UK. It is true that in both countries unemployment has been on an upward trend since the 1960s. Yet, the upward trend is much weaker in the USA, the current unemployment rate being only a little higher than in the 1960s. US unemployment fell sharply between 1982 and 1984, owing to expansionary government budgets, and continued to fall during the 1980s. As in the UK, unemployment in the USA rose in the early 1990s, but much less rapidly. And in both countries, unemployment has fallen recently. The performance of the USA relative to the UK is instructive. Despite having higher unemployment than the UK throughout the 1940s, 50s and 60s, the USA has more recently registered a relatively good unemployment performance. In the 1980s and 90s, it has had much lower unemployment than the UK. The experience of the USA should remind us that no country is destined to remain typified by high rates of unemployment. Chapter 6 continues the comparison of the UK with other countries.

KEY WORDS

Participation	Discouraged workers
Labour Force Survey	Shock
Claimant count figures	

Essay topics

1. In many countries in recent years, large numbers of people have become unemployed. Analyse what causes unemployment and consider the effects of higher rates of unemployment on the economy of a country. [25 marks]

[University of Cambridge Local Examinations Syndicate, 1995]

2. (a) Outline and explain the main changes in unemployment which have occurred in the United Kingdom during the last ten years. [12 marks]
(b) Evaluate the extent to which government policies have influenced the level of unemployment. [13 marks]
[Associated Examining Board 1996]
3. Explain what is meant by full employment and outline the problems of its measurement. Is stable full employment a feasible target for a government? [25 marks]
[Northern Examinations and Assessment Board 1994]

Data Response Question

UK labour force and activity rates
This is based on a question set by the Northern Examinations and Assessment Board in 1993. Study Tables A–G and answer the questions.

1. Describe the changes, actual and projected, in the UK labour force and activity rates as shown in the data.
2. To what extent, if any, do the data suggest reasons for the increased supply of female labour? Answer with reference to economic theory.
3. What are the likely economic consequences of a continued rise in the proportion of female workers in the UK? [40 marks]

Note: Do not attempt to translate all these figures into words. Assume that the reader of your answer has the tables before him or her.

Table A Labour force of working age (thousands)

		1971	1981	1991	2001†
Men aged:	16–19	1054	1363	1111	1091
	20–24	1839	1793	1898	1451
	25–44	6316	6942	7793	7807
	45–64	5820	5211	4795	5402
Total: men		15029	15309	15597	15751
Women aged:	16–19	947	1265	1007	973
	20–24	1241	1412	1600	1293
	25–44	3406	4415	5979	6480
	45–64	2973	2964	3136	3688
Total: women		8567	10056	11722	12434
Total: All		23596	25365	27319	28185

Note: †Projected.

Table B Civilian activity rates (%)*

Men aged:		1971	1981	1991	2001†
Men aged:	16–19	69.4	72.4	73.5	74.6
	20–24	87.7	85.1	85.5	82.6
	25–44	95.3	95.7	94.3	93.9
	45–64	92.0	87.6	80.1	80.2
Women aged:	16–19	65.0	70.4	70.4	70.4
	20–24	60.2	68.8	74.6	77.4
	25–44	52.4	61.7	73.3	79.4
	45–64	58.3	62.9	67.3	67.7

Notes: *Activity rate indicates the proportion of the population of working age in or seeking work. †Projected.

Table C Qualification of school leavers

% leaving with:	Boys			Girls		
	1970	1980	1990	1970	1980	1990
2 or more A-levels	15	15	16	13	13	16
5 or more GCSE/O-levels	7	8	10	9	10	14

Table D Percentage of manual and white collar workers unionized

	1970	1980	1990
Males	52.7	56.4	53.1
Females	31.2	39.5	38.0

Table E Ratio of male to female average hourly earnings excluding overtime

	1970	1980	1990	1991
Full-time manual	1.7	1.4	1.3	1.4
Full-time non-manual	1.9	1.6	1.5	1.5

Table F Percentage share of employment by sector

Sector	1970	1980	1990
Primary	3.6	3.0	1.9
Secondary	46.8	35.6	28.5
Tertiary	49.6	61.4	69.5

Table G Population

Population (millions) aged:	1970	1980	1990	2001†	2011†
0–15	13 469	11 602	11 054	12 041	11 267
16–59	31 686	32 906	34 390	34 922	34 992
60 and over	10 631	11 407	11 911	12 004	13 320
Total	55 786	55 915	57 355	58 967	59 579

Note: †Projected.

Sources: *Monthly Digest of Statistics; Social Trends; Employment Gazette; Trades Union Handbook.*

Chapter Two
Some basic facts about unemployment

'The higher unemployment of the 1980s and 1990s compared with earlier periods is largely due to a growth in long-term unemployment.'

After the last chapter, you may be wondering whether the concept of unemployment means anything at all, and whether in fact we should be worried about it, since it is so difficult to measure. We feel emphatically that unemployment is important and that we should certainly worry about it.

- First, unemployment entails **economic inefficiency.** If 10 per cent of the **labour force** is unemployed, then output is about 10 per cent lower than it could have been, given the amount of goods and services the unemployed could have produced. Further, unlike, say, coal or iron ore, unused labour is lost for ever: it cannot be stored and used later. Unemployment therefore represents an irretrievable waste of our national resources.
- Second, on **equity** grounds, unemployment entails human suffering in terms of low income and low self-esteem.

Consider, first, income. In the 1930s, the income levels on the 'dole' were much lower than today both in real terms and relative to income in work. So, it can be argued that suffering was greater then. Comparing countries today, the incomes of the unemployed (relative to the employed) are lower in the USA than in the UK, but also lower in the UK than elsewhere in Europe.

As regards self-esteem, the effect of unemployment depends a great deal on how long a person has been unemployed. Morale tends to sink progressively during the first six months of unemployment and hardly improves thereafter, however long unemployment continues. People who have been unemployed for more than six months suffer far more each week than those who have been unemployed for two weeks. So it is very important to know how long people have been unemployed.

How long does unemployment last?
The answer in the UK is 'Depressingly long'. Currently, nearly half of all unemployed men have been unemployed for over nine months, and, averaging over all the unemployed, the 'typical' unemployed man has been unemployed for about a year.

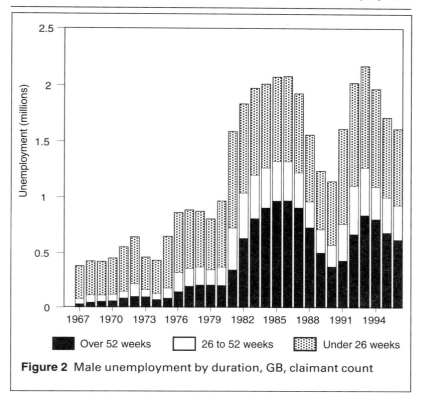

Figure 2 Male unemployment by duration, GB, claimant count

Even more striking, the higher unemployment of the 1980s and 90s compared with earlier periods is largely due to a growth in **long-term unemployment**. *Long-term unemployment means being out of work for over a year.* Figure 2 shows the growth in long-term unemployment. The number of long-term unemployed men in Great Britain rose from 75 000 in 1974 to very nearly a million in 1986. After falling to under 400 000 in 1990, it more than doubled to over 800 000 in 1993 and 1994. By 1996, it had fallen back to 650 000.

There is an important lesson in this rise in long-term unemployment. Changes in the number of long-term unemployed do not result from changes in the numbers becoming unemployed, i.e. from the **inflow** into unemployment. For example, in 1975 and 1985, the number of people becoming unemployed was very similar even though total unemployment rose nearly threefold between these two dates. So why did unemployment rise so much in the 1980s, and why has unemployment stayed so high? It was certainly not because the inflow into unemployment increased. The answer is that people who are becoming unemployed are staying unemployed for much longer. The majority of people now, as earlier, are never unemployed, but those who do become unemployed now suffer much longer unemployment than they used to.

To help us understand what is happening, let us apply a simple rule of thumb. This says that, when unemployment is constant, the number of people who are unemployed at any time equals the number who become unemployed each week times the average number of weeks they remain unemployed:

Number of unemployed = inflow (entrants per week) × average number of weeks unemployed.

By analogy, the number of school students equals the number of first-year students times the length of the course. In the 'school of unemployment', the increased number of students is mainly due not to new entrants but to a depressing increase in the length of the course.

Our formula makes it clear that 10 per cent unemployment could reflect two extreme cases (or anything in between):

- everyone becomes unemployed once a year, for on average 10 per cent of the year; or
- 10 per cent become unemployed each year, for on average a year.

The second extreme case is far closer to the UK situation than the first, and, as we shall see later on, this fact provides an important clue about how to reduce unemployment.

We should concentrate on reducing long-term unemployment, and avoid trying to reduce the proportion of people who become unemployed. For this latter proportion is a powerful force restraining **wage inflation** – *wage inflation is the change in money wages over time* – while long-term unemployment is not and therefore much more of a waste.

Given that long-term unemployment seems to be an important piece of the jigsaw, it is reasonable to ask why it rose by such a large proportion when total unemployment increased. Might this even give us some ideas as to why unemployment has stayed high in the first place? Some suggestive evidence comes from comparing the durations of unemployment in different countries and relating this to their **social security systems** – *that is, the rules defining who gets what benefits and for how long*. As Figure 3 shows, the length of time spent unemployed is very much shorter in Sweden and the USA than in the main European countries.

Why does long-term unemployment vary so much between countries? An obvious factor is again the social security system. In the USA,

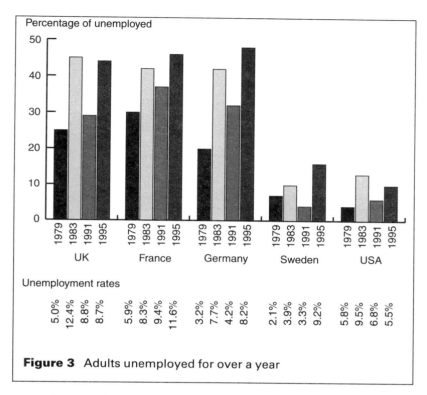

Figure 3 Adults unemployed for over a year

unemployment insurance runs out after six months. After that, in some states, the unemployed get a much reduced income on 'social assistance', but in many states a childless man who has been out of work for over six months gets nothing. In Sweden, benefits last a maximum of 14 months. By then, the unemployed will normally have been offered a place on a training or work programme. Refusing this place results in a loss of all benefit. By contrast, in Germany, benefits continue indefinitely (though at a reduced rate after a year). In France they continue for nearly four years. In the UK, most unemployed people, who receive means-tested Jobseeker's Allowance, have benefits which do not decline, however long they are unemployed.

It is noticeable that countries which have open-ended social security systems not only have high long-term unemployment but also have experienced the largest rises in unemployment. This raises the question of whether countries with open-ended benefits are more likely to develop a culture of unemployment if subjected to a shock (such as the second oil-price rise) which depresses output and employment. Open-ended benefits, which are common in Europe, may reduce incentives for

13

the long-term unemployed to seek work. As a result, it may be more difficult to reduce unemployment in Europe without developing specific measures to deal with the problems of the long-term unemployed.

How do people become unemployed?

In the discussion so far, we have avoided describing the unemployed as *voluntary* or *involuntary*. Unemployment is, of course, affected by individual choices but also by much else besides. Still, it is reasonable to ask how individuals actually come to be unemployed.

The majority of unemployed men have either lost their job through redundancy, left their last job three or more years ago, or never had a job. The proportion of unemployed men who had been made redundant rose markedly at the beginning of the 1990s and has remained at this higher level. In addition, the proportion of unemployed men who have never worked before has been stable at about 10 per cent for each year. Among married women, the proportion leaving a job in the past three years or never having had a full-time job is much smaller. More of them left their last job for family, personal or health reasons, and it is likely that many of these are married women trying to get back to work after child-bearing.

Which occupations, age-groups and regions are most affected in the UK?

It is now time to ask who the unemployed actually are: What are their skills? How old are they? Where do they live, and in which industries did they used to work? The answer is that *the typical unemployed person is low-skilled, young, from the northern half of the UK, and with a background in manufacturing or construction.*

Skills

Let us start with the **skill mix**. In the UK in spring 1996, three-quarters of unemployed men with a previous job were manual workers, and

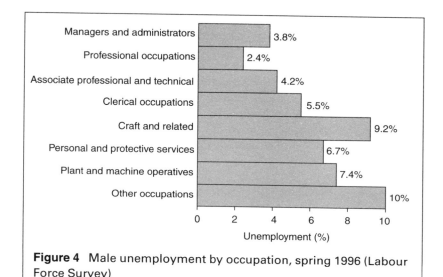

Figure 4 Male unemployment by occupation, spring 1996 (Labour Force Survey)

over half of these were semi-skilled or unskilled. The unemployment rate for non-manual men, 4.8 per cent, is well below half the unemployment rate for manual men, 11.4 per cent. Figure 4 shows unemployment rates by broad occupation.

The difference in unemployment by occupation mainly reflects differences in inflow rates. Duration does not vary much by occupation. The 'Other occupations' in Figure 4 refer mainly to unskilled manual workers, such as labourers, porters and sweepers. The high unemployment rate amongst unskilled male manual workers is nothing new: roughly the same pattern of unemployment rates can be found 20 years ago. Unemployment rates by occupation tend to rise and fall with movements in overall unemployment. However, the relative position of unskilled workers has risen relative to average recently. In winter 1992/93, when unemployment was at a peak the unemployment rate for unskilled male manual workers was 170 per cent of the average unemployment rate for all males. It is now 195 per cent.

Age and unemployment

As Table 3 shows, there is a strong relationship between unemployment and age. Unemployment rates are typically much higher for young people than for older people. The former's higher unemployment rate arises entirely because they are more likely to become unemployed. However, young people who become unemployed do not remain so for as long as older people.

Table 3 Percentage of males unemployed (claimant count) by age, January

	Under 18	18–19	20–24	25–54	55–59	Total
1976	12	11	10	4	5	7
1980	10	11	9	6	6	7
1985	22	29	23	14	19	17
1992	1	20	20	11	12	13
1996	1	20	17	9	9	11

These percentage rates are not comparable over time, but they do indicate relative unemployment by age-group (with the exception of under-18s).

The rise in youth unemployment in the early 1980s was due partly to the general economic situation and partly to the level of youth wages. Job prospects have probably declined more for young people than for others, as employers have cut back on hiring. There have been a number of government responses to the problem of youth unemployment. Since 1979, everyone aged 16 has been guaranteed a place on what was the Youth Opportunity Programme, then became the Youth Training Scheme and is now **Youth Training** (YT). School-leavers are put in training positions, usually for two years, with work experience aimed at training them for a permanent job on completion of the placement. Since 1988, YT has been almost compulsory for unemployed 16- and 17-year olds, as refusing a YT position leads to loss of all benefit entitlement.

The advent of compulsion for the under-18s to join the YT or else lose their benefit makes them invisible in the claimant count. Thus, the claimant count figure for under-18s is extremely low. What happens to young people once this training is finished? Table 3 shows that the ratio of unemployment rates of 18–19 year old men to the average for all men actually worsened between 1985 and 1996. The same is true for 20–24 year-olds. The relative unemployment position of young people has thus worsened over the past eleven years. This suggests that the current youth training schemes are not providing permanent jobs.

International comparisons support the view that pay is a factor in youth unemployment. In Germany, where youth pay is relatively lower than in the UK, youth and adult unemployment rates are about the same. In the UK, a rise in relative youth pay between 1965 and 1975 probably pushed up relative youth unemployment. Yet, since the mid-1980s, the relative pay of youths has fallen quite sharply. Thus, relative pay cannot explain why unemployment among young people in the UK has fallen less than average unemployment over the past eleven years. Possibly, youth unemployment would have risen more without the fall in relative pay. Certainly, factors such as the general economic situation seem more important in recent movements in relative youth unemployment than relative pay.

As we have said, the typical unemployed worker is young, and certainly does not correspond to the common image of the unemployed married man with a large family claiming lots of benefit. In fact, under 40 per cent of unemployed men are married, and only 21 per cent of them have two or more children. Thus, most of them cannot possibly be (unkindly) described as social security scroungers with large families.

Industries and regions

We must now take a look at the industrial and regional aspects of unemployment, which are closely related. We can begin by examining the changing pattern of employees in employment (see Figure 5).

Between 1979 and 1986, manufacturing employment in the UK suffered a devastating decline, falling by 2.5 million – a much higher proportion than in any other country. For every three jobs in manufacturing in 1979, only two remained in 1986. In the same period, however, service employment hardly changed. The subsequent period of recovery from 1986 to 1990 saw stability in manufacturing employment, while service employment increased by nearly 2 million. The recession of 1990 to 1992 again hit manufacturing employment hard and service employment also fell, particularly in Greater London. During the recovery from 1992, service employment again grew while manufacturing employment remained stable. In both recovery and recession periods, employment has shifted from industry to services. This change in the structure of employment is known as **deindustrialization** and it is the subject of a companion volume in this series. Deindustrialization is common to all mature industrial economies, but the UK is exceptional in the severity of the decline in manufacturing employment. This decline hurt some areas more than others, especially the West Midlands and the North of England. Between 1979 and

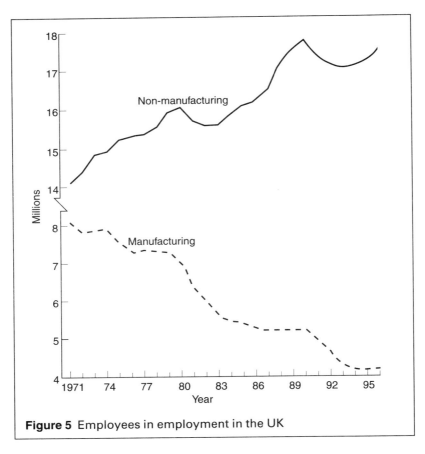

Figure 5 Employees in employment in the UK

1986, unemployment rose more (in terms of percentage points) in those areas which already had high unemployment. In the recession of 1990 to 1992, however, the biggest rises in unemployment were in areas of low unemployment. Chapters 4 and 5 compare these two recessions in more detail.

Looking at the total number of people in employment gives a very incomplete picture of changes in the labour market. Figure 6 shows the workforce in employment (employees plus the self-employed, HM Forces and those on work-related government training programmes).

The workforce has grown faster than the number of employees because it includes the self-employed. Self-employment rose from 1.8 million in 1979 to a peak of 3.5 million in 1990. The right-hand side of Figure 7 shows the growth of self-employment since 1983 for men and women and full-time and part-time workers.

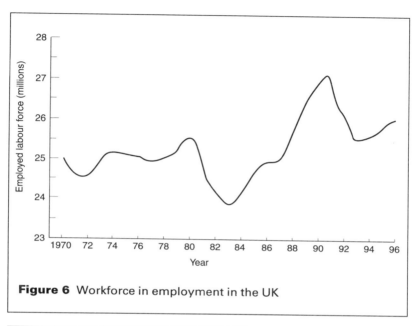

Figure 6 Workforce in employment in the UK

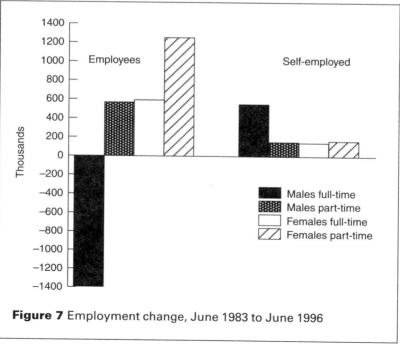

Figure 7 Employment change, June 1983 to June 1996

The growth in male self-employment contrasts sharply with the fall in the number of male employees, shown on the left-hand side of the figure. Whether the growth in male self-employment and male part-time employment is a response to the decline in full-time male jobs is a moot point. The greatest increase has been in female employment, with over 2 million more employees in employment, mainly part-timers, than in 1983. On current trends, by the year 2003 female employees will outnumber male employees.

"HI HO, HI HO, it's off to work we go . . . " chanted the seven dwarfs, as they left Snow White to tend the house, and, of course, to look pretty and vulnerable. These days, it's a fairy tale. The seven dwarfs sit at home, unemployed, lamenting the shortage of jobs for unskilled males – perhaps, for lack of anything to do, turning the pages of the plan released this week by Jacques Delors, president of the European Commission, to revive the European economy and restore full employment. Snow White has no time for such things. She is off to work.

And so it is in the real world. The balance between the sexes in the labour markets of Western Europe and America has changed. Understanding why and how is a crucial first step towards framing an effective policy on unemployment.

Women still account for a lamentably small share of senior jobs; but lower down the ladder, things are different. In Britain, the number of women in work has increased by 18% since the late 1970s, while male employment has fallen by 7%. Britain now has almost as many female employees as male ones, though many are part-timers. In America, too, women have taken the larger share of America's new jobs since the late 1970s. On current trends, a "typical" worker in America and Britain will be a woman by early in the next century.

A main cause of this change is the shift from manufacturing to services. The demand for unskilled, manual labour has slumped: brains are more use than brawn in the new jobs being created in information technology, health, education and other services. This puts women and men on more equal terms than in manufacturing. And for many employers, women workers are a bargain. Often eager for part-time jobs that allow them to combine work with child-rearing, they are willing to work for less. And the flexibility of part-time hours lets firms use labour more efficiently.

The rise in female employment is welcome – both for the new employees and for the economy as a whole. By and large, the new women workers are not taking jobs previously done by men; they are paying taxes and adding to output.

The Economist, 11 December 1993

The jobs that have been created since 1983 are concentrated in the more prosperous southern regions, in the service industries, and include a large proportion of part-time positions. The rise in these jobs that are more attractive to women arguably does little for the 'typical' unemployed worker, who, as was mentioned, has a background in manual work, is male and, as Figure 8 shows, comes from the north of the UK.

In Figure 8, we can see how unemployment rates vary between different regions. These figures, of course, conceal immense variations *within* regions, as some towns have become industrial deserts. There are still whole streets in the North of England (let alone Northern Ireland) where most people are out of work. And even taking quite large travel-to-work areas and using the official registered unemployment figures, there are still some horror stories: Strabane in Northern Ireland, 19 per cent; Cumnock in Scotland, 18 per cent; Aberdare in

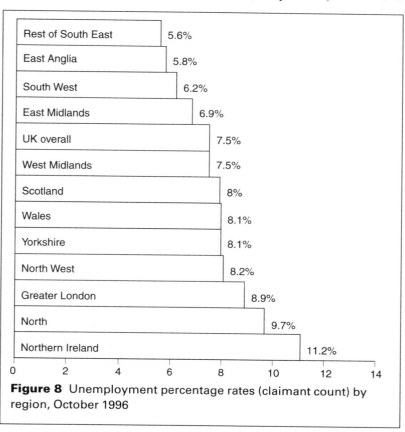

Figure 8 Unemployment percentage rates (claimant count) by region, October 1996

Wales and South Tyneside in North East England (North in Figure 8) both 14 per cent. However, there are also some areas of low unemployment even in regions with above-average unemployment. The two travel-to-work areas with the lowest unemployment in the UK are Clitheroe in North West England and Keswick in Cumbria (North in Figure 8), both with 3 per cent. In Scotland, Aberdeen has the lowest unemployment, under 4 per cent.

The recession of 1990–92 differed from that of the early 1980s in that it hit the South East relatively hard. As a result the differences in **regional unemployment** rates have narrowed noticeably from their levels in the late 1980s. This is discussed further in Chapter 5.

The industrial structure of unemployment (as opposed to that of employment) is not that clear a concept, since only one third of unemployed workers go back to the industry they were in beforehand. However, if we classify the unemployed by the last job they had, then the situation in 1996 was as shown in Figure 9.

Clearly, workers in some industries are always more at risk of unemployment than others owing to the nature of the work that they offer.

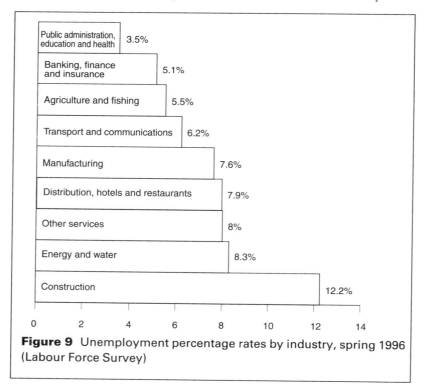

Figure 9 Unemployment percentage rates by industry, spring 1996 (Labour Force Survey)

An obvious example in Figure 9 is construction. Building projects are often short-lived, and workers may be unemployed between projects. (For construction workers, as for young workers, unemployment rates are above average because of high inflow rates rather than longer periods between jobs.) Even so, the fall in employment in the early 1990s hit manufacturing and construction very hard, and construction is still the industry with the highest unemployment rate.

Unemployment and vacancies

Like any other market, the labour market has both buyers and sellers. Up to now, we have concentrated on the sellers – i.e. the employed and the unemployed – but we shall now look at the behaviour of the buyers of labour too.

In the same way that the unemployed can be regarded as frustrated sellers of labour, firms with **vacancies** can be seen as frustrated buyers of labour. Vacancies are advertised in a wide number of ways: at Jobcentres, by private employment agencies, in newspapers, on vacancy boards, by word of mouth, and so on. Exactly how many vacancies exist at any one time is hard to establish precisely. The only reliable information on the number of vacancies available over a reasonable period of time is the number of jobs advertised at Jobcentres. We can use this figure to estimate total vacancies. In autumn 1996, it was estimated that there were:

- 700 000 vacancies in the UK, more than twice as many as in autumn 1992 and roughly the same number as in the late-1980s boom
- 95 000 vacancies in Greater London, four times more than in 1992, a much bigger rise than anywhere else in the UK
- a very similar number of vacancies to the number in the late 1980s in most parts of the UK, including Greater London, which was very hard hit by the early 1990s recession.

700 000 vacancies seems a lot with over 2 million unemployed. The existence of such frustrated supply and demand together suggests a degree of **mismatch** between the vacant jobs and the unemployed. Mismatch is the failure of the skills that the employers demand of new employees to match the skills offered by the unemployed.

Mismatch can also occur for reasons other than skill. The discrepancies between regional unemployment rates are often seen as indicating mismatch, and this situation may be made worse by the cost and difficulty of finding housing in low-unemployment regions.

The labour force and unemployment

Finally, there is an obvious question: can the level of unemployment be explained by the size of the labour force? As a matter of arithmetic we know that:

Unemployment = labour force – employment.

So, if the labour force were smaller in size and employment the same, there would be less unemployment. In a later chapter, we shall argue that over a longish run, unemployment is not going to be affected by the labour force, since if the labour force rises, employment will rise too. That has certainly been the case for most of the past 200 years. But at this stage let us just look at the facts.

Figure 10 shows that the UK labour force grew substantially from 1955 to 1966, with unemployment pretty well stable. The labour force then fell for the next five years but resumed its previous growth rate (except between 1980 and 1983) until the late 1980s. For most of this period since 1966 (of both falling and rising labour force), unemployment rose.

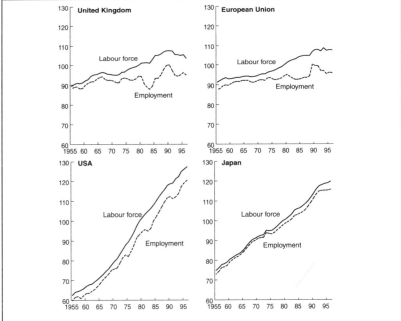

Figure 10 Labour force, employment and unemployment (plotted on a vertical log scale indexed to 1979 = 100)

The contrast with the USA and Japan is striking. In both these countries, the labour force rose much more than in the UK (or Europe); yet unemployment rose much less. We can easily see this by comparing the slopes of the lines in Figure 10.

So why did unemployment rise so much here? In the next chapter, it will be time to make a systematic attempt to find out.

KEY WORDS

Economic inefficiency
Labour force
Equity
Long-term unemployment
Inflow
Wage inflation
Social security system
Skill mix

Youth Training
Deindustrialization
The labour force in
　employment
Regional unemployment
Vacancies
Mismatch

Reading list

Bazen, S., and Thirwall, T., *UK Industrialization and Deindustrialization*, 3rd edn, Heinemann Educational, 1997.

Essay topics

1. (a) Explain why there has been an increase in the proportion of the working population employed in the service sector in the United Kingdom. [12 marks]
   (b) Discuss the economic significance of this change in the pattern of employment [13 marks]
   [Associated Examining Board 1996]
2. (a) How is the rate of unemployment measured in the UK? [6 marks]
   (b) Discuss the extent to which the maintenance of full employment remains a realistic UK macroeconomic policy objective. [14 marks]
   [University of Cambridge Local Examinations Syndicate 1995]

Data Response Question

The changing pattern of employment in the UK
This task is based on a question set by the University of Cambridge Local Examinations Syndicate in 1996. Study Figures A–D, read the following paragraph and answer the questions.

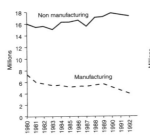

Figure A Manufacturing and non-manu-facturing employees in employment (seasonally adjusted)

Figure B Shares of total employment

Figure C Output of manufacturing indus-tries (Index 1985 = 100)

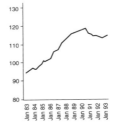

Figure D GDP (Index 1985 = 100)

Since 1980 there has been a considerable change in the pattern of employ-ment in the UK economy with several leading economists expressing concern about the UK's manufacturing sector. There has been much interest in the growth of women's employment, and concern that women's part-time jobs may be replacing full-time jobs for men.

1. (a) Compare the trends in manufacturing and non-manufacturing employment during the period. [1 mark]
   (b) Discuss *two* possible economic consequences of this change in the pattern of employment. [4 marks]
2. (a) What happened to labour productivity in manufacturing industries between 1983 and 1990? Using the data, explain your reasoning. [2 marks]
   (b) Give *two* possible causes of changes in labour productivity. [2 marks]
3. To what extent does the information in Figure B support the view that women's part-time jobs are replacing male full-time jobs? [5 marks]
4. Assuming no increase in the level of population, discuss whether the data indicate an increase in the standard of living between 1983 and 1993. [6 marks]

Chapter Three

The labour market, unemployment and inflation

'If the Treasury were to fill old bottles with bank notes, bury them at suitable depths in disused coal-mines, which are then filled up to the surface with town rubbish, and leave it to private enterprise to dig the notes up again, there need be no more unemployment.' J. M. Keynes

What has gone wrong? Unemployment in the UK and in other European countries over the past 20 years has been very much higher than in the 20 years after 1945. Governments certainly do not want unemployment – it is not good for their re-election prospects. Are they *unable* to reduce unemployment? Or does reducing unemployment conflict with other economic aims more important to governments, such as reducing **inflation**? *Inflation is a rise in the general level of prices. It is often measured by the percentage change in the monthly retail prices index over one year.* (See the companion volume *Inflation and UK monetary policy.*)

Many people see high unemployment as necessary for low inflation. Generally, governments do not justify high unemployment as a deliberate policy choice in this way. They argue instead that low inflation is a necessary condition for future low unemployment. The former Chancellor of the Exchequer Norman Lamont was much criticised for saying the rising unemployment of the early 1990s was a 'price well worth paying' to get inflation down. So, governments *do* use unemployment to control inflation, even if the stated long-run goal is to have low levels of both.

To understand unemployment, we need to understand the relationship between unemployment and inflation. Changes in this relationship do much to explain why unemployment in the past 20 years has been so high. We start our analysis by considering the **labour market**.

The labour market

The labour market can be seen as a market like any other market. Employees and the unemployed sell, or wish to sell, their labour. How many people end up selling their labour and how much labour they wish to sell depends on the market value of their labour, i.e. on the **real**

wage. *The real wage is the actual money wage divided by the general level of prices. It measures the amount of goods and services people can buy with their wages.* So, if money wages and average prices both rise by, say, 5 per cent, the real wage remains the same. The relationship between the amount of labour for sale and the real wage gives **labour supply,** as shown in Figure 11. Employers buy labour, and how much they want to buy will also depend on the real wage. This relationship gives **labour demand.** There is one real wage level at which labour supply and labour demand are equal, that is at which the market clears.

The labour market is not as simple as the figure suggests. There are many **labour market imperfections.** *Imperfections prevent labour supply and labour demand adjusting so as to clear the market.* On the demand side, employers use wages to recruit, retain and motivate their workers, rather than paying a wage which clears the labour market, and trade unions may affect the wage at which labour is supplied. Labour is far from a simple commodity with one clearly established market price. On both the supply and demand sides, the need for information often involves spending time and money before a job-seeker can find employment. The labour market involves long-term commitments which neither employers nor employees wish to disrupt by forcing wages up or down according to labour market conditions. So, for many reasons the labour market is less likely to clear than other markets.

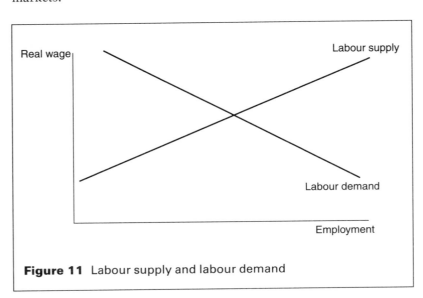

Figure 11 Labour supply and labour demand

Still, the very simple model of the labour market in Figure 11 does suggest one cause of unemployment. Unemployment is labour supply greater than labour demand. This is only possible when the real wage is *above* the market-clearing wage. So, 'too high' wages can cause unemployment. This situation is known as **classical unemployment.**

Classical unemployment assumes that labour demand decides how many people are employed. If there is unemployment, some obstacle on the **supply side** must be preventing the real wage from falling to the market-clearing level. Favourite candidates for supply-side obstacles are trade unions, statutory minimum wages and the social security system. Thus, policies directed at limiting the influence of these obstacles will reduce the real wage and so lower unemployment.

Very different policy solutions can, however, be obtained from the same simple model of the labour market. Rather than the real wage being too high, we could say that labour demand is too low. In this case, the government can act to increase labour demand, for example by spending more or by reducing taxes. Unemployment is then cured by raising the market-clearing wage to equal the current wage, rather than by lowering wages. How the government increases demand does not matter, as the quotation from Keynes at the start of this chapter shows. Unemployment caused by demand being too low is known as **Keynesian unemployment.**

When labour demand and supply are equal, there is **full employment.** This does not mean the absence of unemployment. Even when labour demand and supply are equal, employers still take time to fill vacancies, and job-seekers need time to find work. Unemployment due to the time that unemployed people need to find work when labour supply and demand are equal is known as **frictional unemployment.** *Frictional unemployment is the result of a labour market imperfection, the absence of perfect information. Employers have to spend time obtaining information about job applicants and the unemployed have to spend time finding out about vacancies. The time which vacancies take to be filled results in some people being unemployed.*

The labour market can also be seen as divided into a number of *separate* labour markets, as opposed to the single market shown in Figure 11. For example, the labour market can be seen as two different markets, one for skilled and the other for unskilled workers. If the structure of the economy changes, for example via a shift from manufacturing to services, manufacturing workers who become unemployed may not find it easy or attractive to find work in services. The resulting unemployment of manufacturing workers is an example of **structural unemployment.** Structural unemployment is a slightly different idea from mismatch. It focuses on the last jobs which unemployed people had, whereas mismatch looks at their skills. For a fuller discussion of the labour market, see the companion volume *The UK Labour Market*.

The Phillips curve

The simple model of the labour market in Figure 11 says nothing about inflation. It is a model of real wages. So, inflation should have no effect on unemployment. **The Phillips curve** brings inflation into the picture. It is based on two ideas:

- the Keynesian idea that labour demand explains unemployment
- the idea that labour demand also explains inflation.

If the government raises labour demand so as to reduce unemployment, prices rise. This is because employers find it increasingly difficult to fill vacancies. So, some will start to pay higher wages to attract workers from other employers. As a result, other employers will also pay more because they wish to retain their workers. At the same time, unions will feel in a stronger position to push for wage increases. Higher pay usually translates directly into higher prices because pay is such a large part of employers' total costs. Figure 12 shows the Phillips curve relationship between inflation and employment. If demand is managed so as to reduce unemployment, inflation is higher.

The Phillips curve implies a stable relationship between unemployment and inflation. This notion did not survive the 1970s, when unemployment and inflation rose at the same time (see Figure 14 on page 36). Rising unemployment suggests that the government should raise demand, while rising inflation suggests that it should lower demand. So, the Phillips curve and the belief that unemployment was Keynesian became discredited.

The Phillips curve relationship between unemployment and inflation is wrong in two respects.

- demand determines not inflation but the *change in inflation*
- the equilibrium rate of unemployment over the past 20 years is clearly much higher than in the 20 years after 1945.

We should, then, be looking for a stable relationship between the change in inflation and the difference between actual unemployment and the equilibrium rate of unemployment, where the equilibrium rate of unemployment itself may also change. The relationship between inflation and the actual rate of unemployment is unstable.

The Phillips curve explanation linked the level of unemployment to

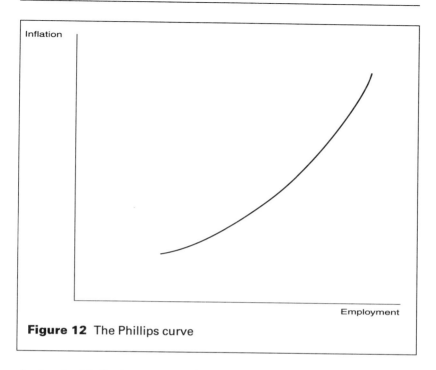

Figure 12 The Phillips curve

the level of inflation. But we have just said that the correct theory should relate the level of unemployment to changes in inflation. Why is this? The answer is that inflation, once present in an economy, has an unpleasant tendency to stay there long after the initial event that produced it has gone away. We can think of the level of prices as being like a body in motion: it moves at the same rate unless acted on by an external force. The difference between the equilibrium rate of unemployment and the actual unemployment rate is the external force which affects the movement of prices. When unemployment is at the equilibrium rate, prices retain their momentum. As a result inflation, the change in prices, shows inertia.

In terms of the model of the labour market given above, imagine that unemployment falls below its equilibrium level, producing a rise in inflation from (for argument's sake) 0 to 5 per cent per annum. For whatever reason, sometime later, unemployment moves back to its equilibrium level. What now happens to prices? The Phillips curve implies that inflation should drop back down again to 0 from 5 per cent. In fact, this doesn't happen: inflation, once implanted, is likely to *continue* at 5 per cent. The reason this happens is that the current rate of inflation plays a decisive role in forming **inflation expectations.**

Inflation expectations

The reason that expectations of inflation are important is that prices and wages do not change continuously unless inflation is extremely high. Price changes usually involve costs, and it is time-consuming to negotiate wages. As a result, prices and wages often stay fixed for some time; wages, for example, are generally negotiated or reviewed only once a year. In fixing prices and wages, firms and unions take account of increases in both costs and prices since the last pay rise, and of likely cost and price rises in the period until the next pay rise, i.e. their inflation expectations. The simplest way of predicting cost and price increases is to look at the current rate of increase, the current rate of inflation. Hence, *price and wage increases almost automatically include the current inflation rate.* This is the reason why inflation tends to carry on at the same rate. When the unemployment rate is not at its equilibrium level, the rate of inflation changes; when the unemployment rate is at its equilibrium level, inflation tends to carry on at the same rate.

The NAIRU

The second reason given above why the Phillips curve does not work is that the equilibrium level of unemployment has itself changed markedly over the past 30 years. The NAIRU is the term many economists use for the equilibrium rate of unemployment. It stands for the **non-accelerating inflation rate of unemployment** – a terrible phrase but one that is preferable to its synonym: the natural rate of unemployment. *When unemployment is at the NAIRU, inflation does not increase. Inflation increases when unemployment is below the NAIRU and falls when it is above the NAIRU.* Governments can always reduce unemployment by raising demand. Unless unemployment is above the NAIRU, reduced unemployment will be at the expense of increasing inflation. Unemployment can only be kept below the NAIRU if inflation continues to increase. This would affect inflation expectations, resulting in accelerating inflation and, in the long run, a collapse of the economy. So, the choice which the Phillips curve implies between inflation and unemployment only holds in the short-run.

How the NAIRU is determined

Economists disagree about the relative importance of market and institutional forces in the labour market, but few, if any, argue that there is anything natural about the levels of unemployment suffered over the past 20 years. In Chapter 8, we examine what government policy can

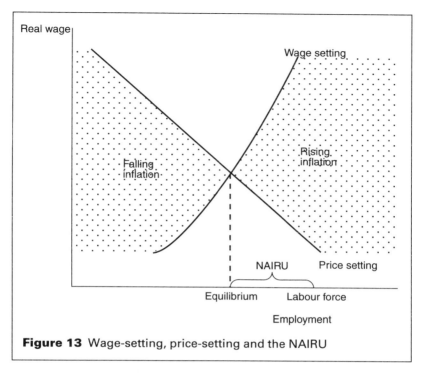

Figure 13 Wage-setting, price-setting and the NAIRU

do to reduce the NAIRU. The institutional forces behind the NAIRU can be seen if, instead of thinking of labour supply, we think of wage-setting and, instead of labour demand, we think of price-setting. These are illustrated in Figure 13.

Wage-setting involves a mark-up of wages above the level of prices to give a **target real wage.** The size of this wage mark-up falls as unemployment rises. Wage-setting often involves bargaining between companies and unions, and unions are more likely to accept lower wages when unemployment is high. High unemployment means low labour demand. This raises the risk of job loss for union members and reduces their chance of finding another job if the current ones are lost. Even without unions, some companies have a target real wage. They need to recruit, retain and motivate suitable workers. Companies' target real wages also fall with unemployment since recruitment, retention and probably also motivation are all easier when workers have fewer alternative job prospects. *Price-setting similarly involves a mark-up of prices above costs,* which we can think of here as wages, to give a **feasible real wage.** Company profits come from the price mark-up. Like the wage mark-up, the price mark-up falls when unemployment rises. High unemployment means low demand, and companies then have to accept lower prices to keep business.

Let us look carefully at what happens if unemployment falls below the NAIRU, perhaps because the government has increased demand. The target real wage rises, while the feasible real wage falls. The actual real wage is somewhere between the target and feasible real wages in the shaded area with unemployment below the NAIRU in Figure 13. Wage-setters seek to increase real wages by raising wages by more than prices, while price-setters seek to lower real wages by raising prices more than wages. As a result, both prices and wages rise by more than the previous rate of inflation. Real wages are higher than companies expected, because they underestimated the rise in money wages when they set prices. So, they reduce employment, bringing unemployment back up to the NAIRU. Once unemployment reaches the NAIRU, the upward pressure on inflation ends. Inflation is therefore stable, but at a higher level than before because of the inertia effect in inflation discussed above. Only rising inflation makes unemployment below the NAIRU possible.

The level of unemployment

The actual level of unemployment may be above or below the NAIRU. So, we can think of unemployment as having two parts, the NAIRU level and the difference from the NAIRU. Unemployment above the NAIRU is often called **overkill**. This reduces inflation. Similarly, unemployment below the NAIRU is known as **underkill**. This, as we have seen, raises inflation. When there is underkill, the economy is unable to supply the goods and services which are being demanded. This pressure on the economy, which pushes up inflation, is called **overheating**.

The short-run and long-run NAIRU

Unemployment can be above the NAIRU for long periods. The NAIRU discussed so far has been the long-run equilibrium rate of unemployment. However, there is also a short-run NAIRU. This reflects the time that the wage- and price-setting process takes to adjust to a change in unemployment. The difference between the short-run and long-run NAIRU depends on how far unemployment is from long-run equilibrium. Until the 1980s, unemployment was close to the long-run NAIRU. So, the distinction between the short-run and long-run NAIRUs probably only became important in the 1980s (see Chapter 4).

The short-run equilibrium level of unemployment depends in part on the current level of unemployment. The short-run NAIRU is a weighted average of the long-run NAIRU and previous levels of unemployment. Even with unemployment above the long-run NAIRU, inflation will rise if unemployment is below the short-run NAIRU. There are three main reasons why unemployment affects the short-run NAIRU.

The first focuses on long-term unemployment. The basic idea is that the long-term unemployed have less effect on wage-setting than the short-term unemployed. The long-term unemployed may well give up hope of finding work, i.e. they may become discouraged workers. This means they effectively stop looking for work. If so, they can have no effect on the labour market or on wage-setting. In the mid-1980s, many of the long-term unemployed did not meet the international definition of unemployment because they were not actively looking for work. In addition, even if they do look for work, employers may consider the long-term unemployed as write-offs, excluding them from the labour market. Thus, an appalling situation can develop in which people are trapped in long-term unemployment: efforts to find work only result in further failure, bringing about an unemployment culture of people who have given up hope. The recession of the early 1980s destroyed many peoples' working patterns and, through high unemployment, undermined the work ethic in large areas of the UK.

The second link between unemployment and the short-run NAIRU is that the labour market is split into **insiders,** who are employed, and **outsiders,** who do not have a job but want one. Wage-setting reflects the interests of insiders, without taking outsiders into account. So, low demand and rising unemployment will affect wage-setting as high wage increases mean that insiders may lose their jobs. Yet, when recovery comes, the increase in demand translates into higher wages, creating few job opportunities for outsiders. If, following a shock, large numbers of workers become unemployed, many may stay unemployed. Wage-setting is not affected by unemployed outsiders. Consequently, wages will not fall when unemployment is high and stable. The insider explanation of high unemployment focuses on the behaviour of employed insiders. It thus differs from the first explanation, which looks at the behaviour of unemployed outsiders and the unwillingness of employers to hire them.

The third link comes from the mismatch between the skills demanded in the economy and the skills possessed by the unemployed. This is something we shall look at in the next chapter, which applies the theory set out in this chapter to the UK.

Unemployment and inflation in practice

To see how reasonable the idea of the NAIRU is, Figure 14 shows the

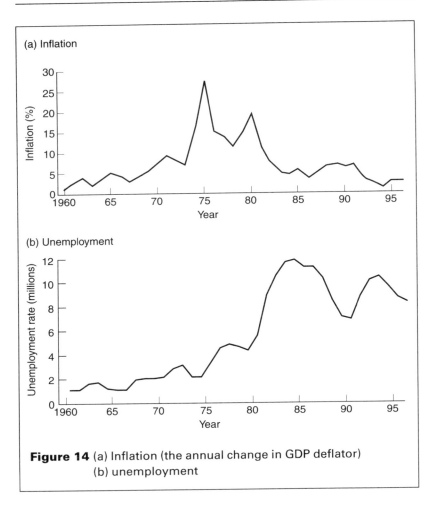

Figure 14 (a) Inflation (the annual change in GDP deflator)
(b) unemployment

history of unemployment and inflation together. Panel (a) shows the inflation rate, and panel (b) the unemployment rate.

Peaks in inflation and troughs in unemployment go together until the 1990s recovery. *Unemployment appears to stop rises in inflation.* As can be seen, inflation tended to rise in the booms of 1961, 1965 and 1970 (all of them related to elections!) when unemployment was lower. On the contrary, in the slacker intervening periods, inflation tended to fall (or rise less) and unemployment was higher. Note that the relationship is not fixed. *As time goes by, more and more unemployment seems to be needed to keep inflation down.* This reflects the rise in the NAIRU discussed above. In the early 1980s, 'overkill' was used to reduce inflation. So, unemployment had to be even higher than the NAIRU. In the early 1990s, unemployment was again raised above the NAIRU, producing a fall in inflation. The fall in unemployment in the 1990s recovery has been less sharp than that in the late 1980s, and it is likely that unemployment has remained above the short-run NAIRU. This explains the relative lack of inflationary pressures in the mid-1990s. The performance of the UK economy is appraised using this model in the next two chapters.

KEY WORDS

Inflation
Labour market
Real wage
Labour supply
Labour demand
Labour market imperfections
Classical unemployment
Supply side
Keynesian unemployment
Full employment
Frictional unemployment
Structural employment

The Phillips curve
Inflation expectations
Non-accelerating inflation rate
   of unemployment (NAIRU)
Target real wage
Feasible real wage
Overkill
Underkill
Overheating
Insiders
Outsiders

Reading list

Heathfield, D. F., and Russell, M., *Inflation and UK Monetary Policy*, 2nd edn, Heinemann Educational, 1996.

Essay topics

1. (a) Why is it difficult to agree what constitutes full employment? [10 marks]
   (b) Discuss the view that imperfections in the labour market are the main cause of unemployment in the United Kingdom. [15 marks]
   [Associated Examining Board 1993]

2. Who gains, and who loses, from:
   (a) inflation [10 marks]
   (b) the effects of anti-inflationary policies? [10 marks]
   [University of Oxford Delegacy of Local Examinations 1994]
3. (a) Explain what is meant by 'the natural rate of unemployment' (also known as NAIRU). [30 marks]
   (b) Evaluate the effects of demand-side and supply-side policies on the natural rate of unemployment [70 marks]
   [University of London Examinations and Assessment Council 1995]

Date Response Question

The labour market, unemployment and inflation

This task is based on a question set by the University of London Examinations and Assessment Council in 1994. Read the article below from *The Economist*, and answer the following questions.

Today's tolerance of unemployment would have astonished people in the 1960s. This week a new book by three British economists considers what the profession has learnt about the subject over the past 20 years. *Unemployment: Macroeconomic Performance and Labour Market* convincingly refutes the idea that countries have no choice but to live with high unemployment.

The macroeconomics of unemployment looks discouraging. The evidence is clear that, for any economy, there is a rate of unemployment that is consistent in the long term with stable inflation. Economists call this the non-accelerating-inflation rate of unemployment, or NAIRU. "There is no long term trade-off between inflation and unemployment", a claim first made by Milton Friedman in the 1960s.

The trouble is that this stable inflation rate of unemployment may well be much too high; it need not correspond to "full employment". The challenge for governments, then, is to change the NAIRU. In the main, this is not a task for demand management, but for supply side policies.

The NAIRU, in effect, is the rate of unemployment that is just sufficient to control pressure for higher wages. It follows that, to lower the NAIRU, governments have to make unemployment more effective – so that a smaller amount of it will exert an equally powerful influence over wage setting. This can be done in several ways. They boil down to one broad idea: the unemployed must become stronger competitors in the labour market.

The new book says that "the unconditional payment of benefits for an indefinite period is clearly a major cause of high European unemployment". In Japan, unemployment benefits stop after six months. Benefits in most European countries are of virtually unlimited duration.

For years, Sweden's labour market policy has been the most successful in Europe. Benefits stop altogether after 14 months, but during that time the unemployed are helped to find work. The means include high quality training courses and recruitment subsidies (including a wage subsidy of up to 50% for those unemployed for more than six months). Sweden spends roughly seven times as much per unemployed worker on such measures as Britain – or roughly 1% of GDP. The net cost to taxpayers is small.

Policies that oblige and equip the unemployed to find jobs will work better if the labour market can be opened up to the new competition. That means scrapping all minimum wage laws. It also means curbing union power. Unemployment is lower if unions and employers co-ordinate their wage bargaining either across industries or nationally.

Source: 'The cursed dole', *The Economist*, 28 September 1991

1. Examine and illustrate what is meant by the phrase, 'There is no long term trade-off between inflation and unemployment'. [5 marks]
2. Explain what is meant when the author states that changing the non-accelerating inflation rate of unemployment 'is not a task for demand management, but for supply side policies'. [4 marks]
3. Using the passage, examine the statement 'the unconditional payment of benefits for an indefinite period is clearly a major cause of high European unemployment'. [4 marks]
4. How can Sweden spend heavily to help the unemployed but find there is only a small net cost to taxpayers? [2 marks]
5. What might be the economic effects of 'scrapping all minimum wage laws'? [5 marks]

Chapter Four
The UK experience

'Being jobless is a price worth paying to beat inflation.'
Former Chancellor of the Exchequer, Norman Lamont

So what is the explanation of our disastrous levels of unemployment in the 1980s and 90s? In the short run, unemployment is determined entirely by the level of spending on British output. Thus, unemployment depends on 'demand'. But demand can be beyond the capacity of the economy to supply output without increasing inflation. So, explaining unemployment in the longer term depends on the 'supply side' of the economy. How much output can the economy supply without increasing inflation? This is where the idea of the NAIRU, explained in Chapter 3, comes in. When unemployment is at the NAIRU, a higher level of demand will still reduce unemployment, but it will also bring in its wake increasing inflation. We shall argue that the rises and falls in unemployment in the 1980s and 90s have been demand-led. In a nutshell, demand factors explain rapid changes in unemployment while the NAIRU explains the level of unemployment over the longer term, with the proviso that it is important to distinguish between the short-run and long-run NAIRU.

Exchange rates, interest rates and government deficits
Three main factors are responsible for changes in demand: interest rates, exchange rates and government deficits.

- The government can use **monetary policy,** the subject of a companion volume in this series, to control interest rates. Yet, using interest rates to lower unemployment may conflict with other policy objectives, such as the rate of inflation.
- **Intervention,** i.e. buying or selling the pound, in the international currency markets affects the pound's value against other currencies, i.e. the exchange rate for the pound. Monetary policy and interest rates also affect the exchange rate. (*UK Trade and Sterling* explains the relationship between interest rates and exchange rates.)
- **Fiscal policy,** also the subject of a companion volume, determines the government's budget deficit. In the early 1980s and 90s, both monetary and fiscal policy were very tight: interest rates were high and budget deficits were being cut.

In the early 1980s, the value of the pound escalated to a level where it became impossible for whole sections of manufacturing industry to sell their goods at all. This was largely due to tight monetary policy resulting in high interest rates. The damage monetary policy did to manufacturing employment is shown in Figure 5 on page 18. For most of the 1980s, the value of the pound meant that British-made goods were much less competitive in comparison with goods made in other countries. Figure 15 shows this loss of competitiveness by looking at an **index of relative unit labour costs** which compares the UK's labour costs per unit of output with a weighted average of its competitors' unit labour costs.

The massive increase in relative costs in the late 1970s and early 1980s was partially reversed in the mid-1980s, which helped the recovery of the late 1980s. This pattern was pretty much repeated in the 1990s. The recession, which took place earlier in the UK than in other countries, was in part caused by the high exchange rate, itself supported by a tight monetary policy. Sterling's ignominious exit from the exchange rate mechanism (see Chapter 5) and the resulting more competitive exchange rate coincided with the 1990s recovery.

Fiscal policy in the 1980s and 90s has reinforced monetary policy, both tending to be either tight or lax at the same time. The biggest

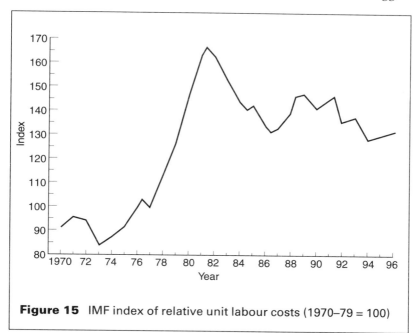

Figure 15 IMF index of relative unit labour costs (1970–79 = 100)

change in fiscal policy came about in the early 1980s. Between 1979 and 1981, the share of taxes in national income was raised from 34 to 38 per cent, while government expenditure (as a percentage of potential output) remained virtually unchanged. Similar squeezes happened in other major European countries, but the reverse happened in the USA. This provides a perfectly controlled experiment for the effect of fiscal policy. *Between 1979 and 1986, the budget deficit in the UK and other European Union countries was cut by 4–5 per cent of national income. In the European Union, unemployment by 1986 was more than 5 per cent higher than in 1979. By contrast, in the USA, the budget deficit was expanded, and there was no rise in unemployment compared with 1979.* More recently, concerted efforts have been made by a number of European countries to cut budget deficits to meet the Maastricht criteria for the single European currency. Again, the unemployment performance of the countries enforcing the most swingeing cuts has been at odds with those (such as the UK) where the fall in the deficit has been less marked. *These examples show the power of fiscal policy to influence the level of unemployment.*

The golden age

The 20 years from 1945 were a 'golden age' for unemployment, which averaged 1.6 per cent – much lower than ever before or after. In this period, demand management proved to be a solution to Keynesian unemployment. However, in the 1960s, unemployment and inflation showed a tendency to rise, although both remained at relatively low levels (see Figure 14 on page 36). Governments managed demand to deal with periodic balance-of-trade difficulties, as well as to keep unemployment down. With fixed exchange rates, high demand led to both trade deficits and increases in inflation. The rise in inflation was small. So, unemployment was close to the NAIRU. At the same time, the NAIRU itself was creeping up for a variety of reasons. The most important of these reasons included:

* greater union pressure
* decentralization of pay bargaining
* wider access to the social security system, and
* higher taxes on jobs (a rise in employers' National Insurance contributions).

The 1960s and 1970s: The failure of demand management

By the 1960s, governments were less and less able to use demand management to ensure low unemployment without increasing inflation. The rise in the NAIRU meant that inflation could only be stable with higher unemployment than in the past. To try to maintain low unemployment without increasing inflation. Governments intervened directly to influence pay increases. Governments reached agreements with the trade unions on pay restraint or introduced legal controls over pay increases. In terms of the NAIRU, the price-setting relationship was affected. Higher non-wage costs meant that the price mark-up over wages for any level of unemployment rose, reducing the feasible real wage. In the early and mid-1970s, governments sought to keep unemployment below the NAIRU. Inflation soared, reaching a peak of 27 per cent a year in 1975.

1975–79: The success and failure of incomes policy

This inflationary crisis led to an agreement between the government and the trade unions on a drastic incomes policy limiting pay increases to £6 a week (about 10 per cent for the average worker). The policy was a dramatic success, reducing inflation to 14 per cent in 1976. Trade union support for incomes policy ended in 1978 when the government sought a 5 per cent limit. The resulting disagreement over pay between unions and government, which followed a partial economic recovery, led to a series of strikes in the so-called 'Winter of Discontent' in 1978/79.

1979–85: A costly solution

The Conservative government elected in 1979 faced the same problems as did the Labour government in 1974: a large oil price rise and the collapse of its predecessor's incomes policy. Its solution, however, was very different. This time, the inflationary fire was put out by a huge dose of unemployment, driven by contractionary monetary and fiscal policy. Lower government spending, high interest rates and an appreciation of the exchange rate reduced demand and increased unemployment. In 1979, unemployment was only 4 per cent, about $2\frac{1}{2}$ per cent above the level of the 1950s and early 1960s. But after 1979, unemployment rose rapidly to over 10 per cent, a far bigger increase. As a result, the economy was in the area of falling inflation shown in Figure 13 on page 33. With unemployment now above the NAIRU, inflation fell. This policy had enormous costs: between 1979 and 1981, national output fell by 5 per cent, more than in any other industrial country. The prolonged recession of the early 1980s meant a build up of long-term unemployment (see Figure 2 on page 11). This increased the short-run NAIRU. The economy started to grow again in 1981, but unemployment continued rising until 1986. The rise in unemployment in the early 1980s was concentrated in areas and occupations where it was already high – the recession was very inegalitarian.

For most of the 1980s, unemployment was well above the long-run NAIRU, but probably not much above the short-run NAIRU. This explains why the high level of unemployment had only a small effect on pay increases. Through the mid-1980s, pay increases were very stable at around $7\frac{1}{2}$ per cent. But despite this, inflation fell to a low of less than $2\frac{1}{2}$ per cent in mid-1986. This fall in inflation owes more to price-setting than to wage-setting. There was a 'third oil price shock' – but a fall this time. The fall in oil and commodity prices increased the feasible real wage and thus reduced the NAIRU. This price shock probably had a greater effect on inflation than did an unemployment rate which, although high, was still quite close to the short-run NAIRU.

1986–89: An unsustainable recovery

Demand expanded rapidly from 1985. Initially, this was not a direct result of government policy, but a consequence of financial deregulation, which made borrowing much easier for consumers (see *UK Current Economic Policy* in this series for details). A recovery in investment (albeit from a low level) also played a part in the expansion of demand. National output grew on average by an unprecedented 4.1 per cent a year between 1985 and 1988. In 1988, the government further increased demand with large tax cuts. Unemployment was almost halved between 1986 and 1990, with the claimant count rate falling from 11 per cent of the labour force to less than 6 per cent. The improvement in the labour market that this fall signals was not shared equally by all. First, the figures conceal a large rise in the number of people on work-related government training programmes from just 8 000 in June 1983 to 376 000 in September 1988. Second, there was evidence of substantial mismatch between the type of workers who were unemployed and the type of jobs that this recovery created. The new jobs of the late 1980s were concentrated in the more prosperous southern regions, in the service industries, and included a large proportion of part-time positions. The rise in these types of jobs can be argued to do little for the 'typical' unemployed worker of Chapter 2, who has a background in industry, is male and comes from the north of the UK. By the late 1980s, unemployment had certainly dropped below the short-run NAIRU (although it may still have been above the long-run NAIRU); in consequence, inflation rose once again.

The 1990s continue trends of the 1980s

Chapter 5 examines the government's response to the resurgence of inflation and looks in detail at unemployment in the 1990s. Many of the trends of the 1980s continued into the 90s. For example, in looking at the changing structure of employment in Figures 5, 6 and 7 we did not distinguish the 1980s from the 1990s. For **active labour market policy**, it also makes sense to consider the 1980s and 90s together. Active labour market policy is the name given to a wide range of government measures for dealing with unemployment other than the passive labour market policy of providing income for the unemployed through the benefit system.

Active labour market policy

Active labour market policy covers a wide range of programmes and activities. The most important are assistance with job placement through Jobcentres, training for the unemployed, including measures to assist effective job search, and employment subsidies, such as payments to employers to recruit unemployed people or to the unemployed to encourage them to become self-employed. Active labour market policy is one aspect of **supply side economics**, also the subject of a companion volume. It aims to ensure that the unemployed are an effective part of the economy's labour supply.

In the early 1980s spending on active labour market policy fell sharply in relation to the numbers unemployed. This fall in spending was only in part due to the large increase in unemployment. The government relaxed the requirement for unemployed people to sign on as seeking work as a condition of receiving benefit. This probably contributed to a decline in search effectiveness, particularly of the long-term unemployed. Many of the long-term unemployed did not satisfy the international definition of seeking work. As a result, in the early 1980s, the numbers unemployed on the claimant count were actually more than on the international definition.

Since 1986, when Restart interviews were introduced, the Employment Service has developed a number of valuable measures to advise and motivate the unemployed to search effectively for work. The Restart interview is compulsory after six months' unemployment. Claimants explore all the possibilities open to them with an advisor. The interview now includes updating the Back to Work Plan, which claimants agree when they first sign on. A variety of schemes are open

Makework

Since you cannot hear a hyphen, it was unclear whether Peter Lilley, the social security minister, was appealing in his conference speech this week in Bournemouth to the "hard-working classes" or the "hard working-classes". Both, probably; for this is the latest term for Essex man, Sierra man, the C2s whom the Tories fear they are losing to Labour. The swathe of employment and social-security measures announced or implemented this week is intended to persuade these people that the Tories are against dole-scroungers while Labour is in favour of them. On close inspection, however, they reveal more similarities than differences. The changes fall into broad categories:

- Cutting costs. The new Jobseeker's Allowance, introduced by the government on October 7th, cuts the period of time for which the newly-unemployed get unconditional benefits from a year to six months. At the end of six months, those who have more than £4,000 in savings, or whose partner is working, will get no more benefits.
- Project Work neatly illustrates the degree of consensus between the two main parties on the direction that future welfare reform should take. Workfare – no work, no benefits – is designed to do three things: to eliminate from the unemployment register those who are working on the black; to prevent the lazy from sitting on their backsides at the taxpayer's expense; and to reconnect the long-term unemployed with the world of work.

Project Work caters to people who have been out of work for more than two years. During the first 13 weeks, which are voluntary, it offers them help with looking for a job: the unemployed person gets a fortnightly session with an adviser, who will help with applications and phone employers. The next 13 weeks are compulsory: 18 hours of work a week with a voluntary organisation. Those who refuse to do it lose their benefits. The scheme runs from April 1996 to July 1997.

The scheme is not perfect. Richard Layard, an economist at the London School of Economics who has written extensively on the subject, reckons that a workforce scheme has a better chance of succeeding if it gets people before they have been out of work for so long; and he doubts that the compulsory period is long enough. "It doesn't seem at all serious."

...Early figures suggest that Project Work may be doing its stuff. According to Sandy Tulloch, district manager in Hull for the Employment Service, only 40% of those on the scheme wanted the initial 13 weeks' help in looking for work. Of the 2,100 people who have been through the project only 182 have found jobs. However, 475 have come off the register altogether. Presumably they had pressing engagements elsewhere. At that rate, the scheme should easily repay the £6m it will cost for the 4,500 people who will go through it in Hull.

This tough-minded approach to welfare may well prove effective. Yet the Tories cannot claim sole ownership. Labour, after all, is offering a more expensive version of the same thing: unemployed people under 25, Labour has promised, will be offered a job or more education, and if they refuse they will lose their benefits. Hard for the non-working classes; but appealing to the hard-working classes.

The Economist, 12 October 1996

to claimants. As well as the training and enterprise schemes covered in the next paragraph, there are a number of schemes which aim to improve job seeking skills. For example, Workwise is a four-week course on jobsearch for 18–24 year olds who have been unemployed for over a year. Some claimants are given a Job Interview Guarantee after a one-week Job Preparation Course. Employers agree to interview people whom the Employment Service has selected according to their individual requirements.

The government introduced four 'new' training and enterprise schemes in 1993. These schemes were largely a case of old wine in new bottles – a change of label, but not of content. For example, Training for Work replaced Employment Training as the main label for training schemes for the unemployed. The changing labels conceal continuity. For most of the 1980s and 90s, the unemployed have had access to three types of scheme: training schemes, work experience schemes and subsidies to self-employment. The quality of training available has, however, varied considerably. From 1972 to 1985, the Training Opportunities Scheme gave the unemployed the chance of high-quality training. Currently, the unemployed have little access to high-quality training. However, lower-quality training has the advantage of enabling mass training without greatly increased expenditure on active labour market policy. From 1988 to 1991, Employment Training was the largest-scale training attempted in the UK. Work experience does not involve any training, but aims simply to give the unemployed something useful to do. Employment subsidies were introduced on a small scale in 1995. Previously, the government had only subsidized self-employment. The objective of these subsidies is to encourage employers to recruit the long-term unemployed.

Under the 1989 Social Security Act, the government adopted a more coercive approach to claimants. Receipt of benefit for unemployment was made conditional on 'actively seeking work'. Previously, benefit claimants were only required to be capable and available for suitable work. The new 'actively seeking work' provision may seem a radical change, but it was merely the fourth instalment of a progressive tightening of conditions for benefit in the 1980s. In 1982, availability for work tests had been made stricter, and in 1986, after a National Audit Commission report suggesting that the 1982 changes were ineffectual, the questionnaire for new claimants was changed to test availability more rigorously. From 1988, Restart interviews have included a formal check on availability. The danger of excessive coercion here is that the unemployed are likely to see all interviews as just one more hurdle to jump to obtain benefit and not as an effort to provide assistance and advice on how best to go about getting work. A programme in which the unemployed participate on pain of loss of benefit will be much less effective than if they had *chosen* to participate. Employment Service staff are much less likely to explain the benefits of a compulsory programme. They simply need to inform claimants that non-participation results in loss of benefit. Research carried out for the government has consistently shown that lack of information is a major reason why government schemes have low entry rates and high drop-out rates.

The Jobseekers Act, which came into effect in October 1996, dramatically increased compulsion. The unemployed need to provide written details of jobseeking. For a significant proportion of the unemployed, this could be a valuable exercise since it encourages the unemployed to maintain a high level of job search and can also be useful in reviewing methods of job search. Yet, it is not sensible to compel every unemployed person to give written details of employers contacted in the knowledge that benefit may be lost if the expected number of contacts are not made. Since the information cannot be checked, such compulsion merely camouflages fraudulent claims and penalizes honesty. The central fallacy of the Jobseekers Act, and of similar measures on 'actively seeking work' which preceded it, is the supposition that activities which promote job-finding when undertaken voluntarily have the same effect when obligatory.

An element of coercion is necessary for any system of benefit for the unemployed. Benefit should not be used to support indolence or supplement earnings in the black economy, however inadequate these might be. Coercion in the form of penalties for abusing the system is essential. Yet, if the unemployed experience the approach of the Employment Service as coercive, they are more likely to become demoralized and less likely to be motivated job seekers.

KEY WORDS

Monetary policy	Index of relative unit labour
Intervention	costs
Fiscal policy	Supply side economics
Active labour market policy	

Reading list

Cook, M., and Healey, N., *Supply Side Economics*, 3rd edn, Heinemann Educational, 1996.

Essay topics

1. (a) How is the performance of an economy affected by *both* the geographical and the occupational mobility of labour? [12 marks]
   (b) Outline the various ways in which the government can seek to improve the mobility of labour, and critically evaluate the arguments for and against such intervention by the government. [13 marks]
   [Associated Examining Board 1996]

2. Explain how the use of a reflationary fiscal policy may influence:
   (a) the level of aggregate demand [40 marks]
   (b) the level of unemployment [30 marks]
   (c) the aggregate price level. [30 marks]
   [University of London Examinations and Assessment Council 1994]

3. (a) An open economy is currently operating well inside its production possibility curve. Explain the likely consequences for this economy of a cut in interest rates. [10 marks]
   (b) Why might a government allow significant levels of unemployment to exist? [10 marks]
   [University of Cambridge Local Examinations Syndicate 1996]

4. 'Controlling inflation is easy. Controlling inflation whilst maintaining a high level of employment is impossible.' Discuss, in the light of recent United Kingdom experience. [25 marks]
   [University of Oxford Delegacy of Local Examinations 1995]

Data Response Question

Unemployment, inflation and savings

This task is based on a question set by the University of London Examinations and Assessment Council in 1995. Study Figures A, B and C, and answer the questions.

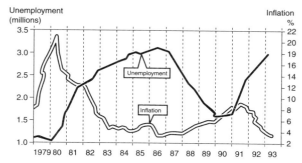

Figure A Unemployment and inflation

Source: *The Times,* 22 February 1993

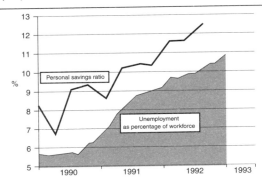

Figure B Unemployment and savings

Source: *The Sunday Times,* 21 February 1993

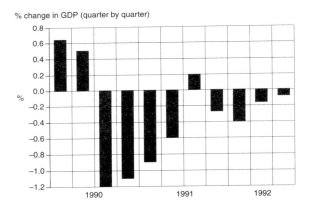

Figure C Growth and recession

Source: G. Cook, *Economics Update* 1993, Sterling Books

1. Using the data from both Figures A and B, estimate the size of the labour force at the end of 1992. Show your calculations. [3 marks]
2. (a) What does Figure A suggest about the relationship between inflation and unemployment? [3 marks]
   (b) Using economic analysis, explain the relationship which you have identified in (a). [5 marks]
   (c) Mr Norman Lamont (then Chancellor of the Exchequer) said in May 1991 that unemployment was 'a price worth paying in order to achieve a low rate of inflation'. In the light of this statement, examine *two* benefits of a low rate of inflation. [4 marks]
3. Examine possible reasons which might explain the movement of the personal savings ratio between 1990 and 1992. [5 marks]

Chapter Five

UK unemployment in the 1990s

'The government then sent for the fire brigade in the form of higher unemployment.'

By 1988, it was clear that the economy could not continue its rapid growth. The boom had once again ignited inflation. The government finally accepted that the party could not continue. *It sent for the fire brigade in the form of higher unemployment.* The government pushed up interest rates, doubling the **base rate** from $7\frac{1}{2}$ per cent in May 1988 to 15 per cent in October 1989. This very high level continued for another year. The high level of consumer borrowing in the late 1980s made the rise in interest rates a particularly potent weapon in the deflationary war. High interest rates also pushed up the value of the pound, as in the early 1980s (the companion volume *UK Trade and Sterling* explains how interest rates affect the exchange rate). The government sought to make the high exchange rate permanent by entering the **exchange rate mechanism** in October 1990 (see the companion volume *The European Union* for details on the ERM).

The fall in unemployment, which had started in 1986, ended in April 1990. This chapter applies the analysis developed in Chapter 3 to the subsequent behaviour of unemployment in the 1990s. First, we set out the basic facts which we have to explain. In doing so, we shall compare the recession of the early 1990s with the previous recession of the early 1980s. This will allow us to assess the effects of the radical policies of the 1980s on the workings of the labour market.

The basic facts

The movements in employment and unemployment from 1990 to 1996 are set out in Table 4, which uses the claimant-count definition of unemployment. (On the international definition, the rise in unemployment between 1990 and 1993 is greater and the fall between 1993 and 1996 is smaller).

Table 4 Employment and unemployment 1990–96 (seasonally adjusted)

	June 1990 (millions)	June 1993 (millions)	June 1996 (millions)	Percentage change 1990–93	Percentage change 1993–96
Employees in employment:					
Manufacturing	5.1	4.4	4.3	−14.7	− 0.9
Services	15.9	15.7	16.4	− 1.8	+ 4.8
Other sectors	1.8	1.5	1.4	−20.1	− 5.9
All employees	22.9	21.5	22.1	− 6.1	+ 2.9
Self–employed	3.5	3.2	3.3	−10.1	+ 3.7
HM forces	0.3	0.3	0.2	−11.4	−18.5
Unemployed and government training schemes	2.0	3.2	2.4	+58.8	−27.2
Labour force	28.8	28.2	28.0	− 2.1	−0.7

Note: The other sectors are building, farming and energy.

The rise in unemployment from 1990 to 1993

The early 1990s initially appear very similar to the early 1980s. The largest contributions to the rise in unemployment again came from the decline of manufacturing and the loss of jobs in the building industry, which always suffers severely in recessions.

What happened to unemployment

The rise in unemployment in the 1990s was, in fact, very different from that in the 1980s, particularly in its regional distribution. This is shown in Figure 16, which compares the last two periods of rising unemployment. In the early and mid-1980s, unemployment increased the most in regions of high unemployment. The biggest exception is the West Midlands, which had almost the highest rise in unemployment despite starting the recession with below-average unemployment. This is due to the importance of manufacturing to the West Midlands economy. In contrast, the regions which recorded the largest rise in unemployment in the 1990s recession were those where the rate of unemployment was lowest.

The most striking point about the rise in unemployment in the recession of the early 1990s is that it occurred to a greater extent in areas with initially low rates of unemployment. The contrast between the

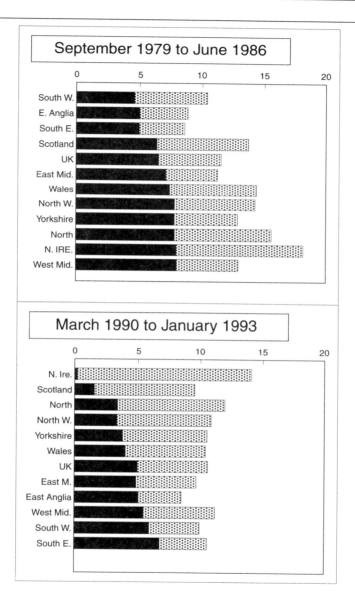

Figure 16 Increases in unemployment by region 1979–1986 and 1990–93

Note: The claimant count does not give a good measure of the level of unemployment, but it does indicate the relative trends in different parts of the UK.

regions of low and high unemployment is even more marked when one considers the increase in unemployment from March 1990 to January 1993 as a percentage of its level in March 1990. This figure ranges from 4 per cent in Northern Ireland and 20 per cent in Scotland to 150 per cent in the South West and East Anglia, and an amazing 190 per cent in the South East, including London. By way of contrast, in the recession of the early 1980s, the rise in unemployment was generally higher in regions where unemployment was already high. Thus, the early-1990s recession was much more egalitarian than that of the 1980s in that regional differences in unemployment rates faded rather than sharpened.

Unemployment in the early 1990s rose rather less than in the early 1980s, while vacancies fell more sharply than ten years earlier. In fact, the levels of both unemployment and vacancies in 1992, as well as the ratio of unemployment to vacancies, were very similar to those which prevailed in 1982. So, there were roughly as many unemployed then as there were a decade earlier, and each unemployed person had about the same chance of finding a vacancy then as they did ten years earlier. Vacancies and unemployment increased together in both 1983 and 1993. However, the rise in unemployment in 1993 was much less than in 1983. In the mid-1990s, unemployment fell steadily, while in the mid-1980s it continued to rise slowly until the middle of 1986.

What happened to employment

The varied changes in unemployment in the different regions of the UK in the early 1990s were largely driven by changes in service employment. While employment in manufacturing and other sectors declined in every region, service employment was hit severely in the South East but grew significantly in Scotland, the East Midlands and East Anglia. This again contrasts sharply with the early 1980s, when the decline in manufacturing relative to other employment, see Figure 5 on page 19, accounted for much of the change in employment in the UK, and indeed for much of the regional variation in the growth of unemployment. For example, the West Midlands had the largest absolute rise in unemployment, reflecting the concentration of manufacturing in that region.

Self-employment

Between 1990 and 1993, self-employment fell by nearly 400 000 (see Table 5), and this is another contrast with the early 1980s. The 1980s recession did not interrupt the growth in self-employment which lasted from 1977 to 1990. The regional variation in self-employment in the early 1990s was similar to that for services employment. In the South East, the fall in self-employment made a significant contribution to the rise in unemployment. The fall in self-employment in the South East in the three years to 1993 was equivalent to 2 per cent of the total labour force. In contrast, self-employment in Scotland and Northern Ireland rose by an amount equal to about 1 per cent of the labour force.

Reasons for the rise in unemployment

Unemployment, at its peak in January 1993, reached 3 062 065, according to the claimant count. Seasonally adjusted, the rise from March 1990 was almost 1.4 million. (The seasonally-adjusted figure in January 1993 was 7 000 short of 3 million.) For the economics of this rise in unemployment, we must, as usual, look at both demand and supply developments.

Demand side forces

When unemployment increases rapidly, it is natural to look first at the demand side for the explanation. Supply side factors, which determine the NAIRU, tend not to fluctuate sharply. The two obvious factors which affected real aggregate demand were the exchange rate and interest rates.

On the exchange rate side, the pound entered the European Union's exchange rate mechanism (ERM) in October 1990. The central banks of EU member countries are committed to maintaining the exchange rate of each currency within fixed bands. One way in which central banks can affect exchange rates is by purchasing or selling currencies on the foreign exchange market. Of greater importance for our analysis of unemployment is the restriction that EU membership imposes on interest rates in member countries. Interest rates must be such that there is sufficient demand for each currency from investors to keep the currencies within their respective ERM bands.

The exchange rate chosen for sterling within the ERM appeared to be such that interest rates had to be maintained at a high level in order to support the currency. The British economy in the early 1990s thus faced the same combination of high exchange rates and high interest rates as it did in the early 1980s. The effect of this combination was to curtail the demand for UK goods. A strong exchange rate ensured that goods from the UK were expensive in other countries (although it also delivered benefits in terms of lower prices for imported goods, helping to reduce the rate of inflation). At the same time, high domestic interest rates dampened domestic demand on the part of both firms and consumers. Consumer demand in the 1990s is especially responsive to the level of interest rates because individuals have borrowed more money to buy consumption goods, and because so many individuals are tied to floating-rate mortgages as a result of the boom in home ownership in the 1980s.

By September 1992, it became clear that a weakening pound could not stay within its required band against the deutschmark. In a market where trade in goods and services is only responsible for 10 per cent of transactions, a belief that the value of sterling would fall was enough to bring about massive sales of the currency. The UK government purchased sterling on the market and raised interest rates, but it was not enough to prevent the pound from dropping through its ERM floor and then being withdrawn from the ERM system.

After its exit from the ERM, the pound floated at a level of around DM2.50, which represents a devaluation of 15 per cent from its previous ERM parity. While this devaluation raised fears of inflation (due to dearer imports) for some in the government, the Chancellor of the Exchequer welcomed the chance to use the floating exchange rate as part of 'a British economic policy and a British monetary policy'.

Entry into the ERM had not meant a change in policy on interest rates and the exchange rate. This policy had been adopted in response to clear signs of overheating in the economy in the late 1980s. The two obvious signs of overheating were a rise in inflation and a rise in the balance-of-trade deficit. Overheating occurs when unemployment is less than the NAIRU (i.e. where there is 'underkill') (see Chapter 3).

Supply side factors
Developments in the level of aggregate demand can explain the rise in unemployment in the 1990s. However, the long-run level of unemployment must, as always, be explained on the supply side. Why did overheating occur in the late 1980s?

Unemployment at the end of the boom was only just below 7 per cent on the Labour Force Survey measure. At this point, the level of demand was clearly above the economy's short-term capacity to supply, as was shown by the rising rate of inflation and the increase in the balance-of-trade deficit. *This suggests that the NAIRU is significantly more than 7 per cent.* The NAIRU of the early 1990s did not seem to be much different from that of the early 1980s. At first sight, this is extremely disappointing in view of the supply side policy measures which we outlined in Chapter 4.

Making companies efficient
The year downsizing grew up

...The past decade has seen downsizing evolve from an act of desperation into a calculated choice. The first downsizers were failing companies: many of them had no choice but to go in for repeated bloodlettings as their business shrank and morale collapsed. But more recently a new sort of company has taken up the practice: successful firms that use job-cutting as a way to pursue a wider purpose.

...The transformation of downsizing is the result of two trends in management thinking. One is the realisation that size in itself is no longer a source of competitive advantage. The past decade has seen the humbling of a series of giants.

...Rather than celebrating their size, big companies have taken to hiding it; they try to imitate the agility of their smaller rivals by shrinking their headquarters, slashing away layers of management and breaking themselves up into smaller units. Some have gone the whole hog and broken themselves up into separate companies.

...The other new management fashion is to focus on your "core competences": the things that you – and you alone – can do better than anyone else.

...The language of downsizing is a nasty mix of pseudo-science and euphemism. These days you can be "rightsized", "displaced", even "put into the mobility pool". The reality is wrenching, even for those who have the luck to jump to another well-paid job. And some of the consultants who make a living from the business have all the moral dignity of ambulance-chasing lawyers. But European and Japanese managers will have to learn to live with downsizing over the next decade or so. Studying the American experience, however distasteful much of it sounds, makes better sense than flying by the seat of your pants.

The Economist, 21 December 1996

The fall in unemployment from 1993
Two very different recoveries

The 1990s recovery contrasts in two respects with the 1980s recovery. Unemployment started to fall much earlier in the recovery, and wages grew more slowly. Part of the explanation for the difference between the two recoveries is that, as Figure 16 shows, regional imbalances in the 1990s were less than in the 1980s. Also, the labour force grew less rapidly in the 1990s than in the 1980s. The labour force figures may,

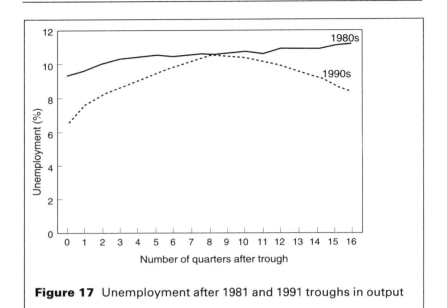

Figure 17 Unemployment after 1981 and 1991 troughs in output

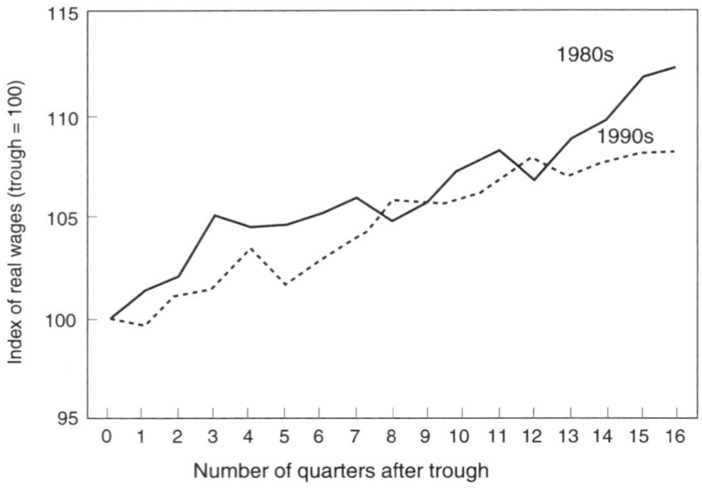

Figure 18 Rises in real wages after 1981 and 1991 troughs in output

however, be misleading because more people are receiving benefit because they are unable to work. The increase in the number of students at colleges and universities is another factor holding back the growth in the labour force in the 1990s. This has potentially a large effect on unemployment as young workers are more likely to be unemployed. Yet, even allowing for all these factors, *the 1990s recovery still suggests a reduction in the NAIRU.*

Once output started to rise again, unemployment fell much sooner in the 1990s than it had in the 1980s. This is shown in Figure 17 for the periods since the troughs in real gross domestic product. The troughs were in the first quarter of 1991 and the second quarter of 1981.

Another difference between the two recoveries is the behaviour of real wages. In the three years after each trough, real gross domestic product rose by about $8\frac{1}{2}$ per cent. So, if wage-setting behaviour in the early and mid 1990s was the same as a decade earlier, similar increases in real wages would be expected. Figure 18 compares rises in real wages in the four years after each trough.

In the 1990s, real wages grew much less rapidly than in the 1980s. Recently, however, real wages show some signs of faster growth. As a result of this rise in wages and other signs of increasing inflation, the government raised interest rates in October 1996. In October 1996 unemployment, even on the claimant-count figures, was $7\frac{1}{2}$ per cent, significantly more than in the late 1980s. So, the government did not appear to think that it has reduced the NAIRU much. One reason for the failure of the NAIRU to fall is the resurgence of regional mismatch (see the box on page 60).

The success and failure of employment policies

We said above that the NAIRU in the late 1980s did not seem to be much different from that at the beginning of the decade. Does this reflect the failure of the supply side labour-market policies undertaken throughout the 1980s? Although at first sight it does seem to do so, supply side measures may still have been successful in preventing an increase in the short-run NAIRU as a result of the very high unemployment of the early 1990s. High unemployment generally means that the proportion of the long-term unemployed increases. As explained in Chapter 3, the long-term unemployed may give up hope of employment and stop looking for work effectively. Moreover, as we saw, employers may be unwilling to employ them, particularly if they can easily recruit workers who are not suffering from long-term unemployment. For these reasons, the long-term unemployed are less effective than the short-term unemployed in searching for work and so play a smaller role in restraining wage inflation.

Boom in the south puts north behind

...One of the big economic stories of the 1980s was the lopsided regional nature of activity. It began with the first Thatcher recession of 1980–81, which hit manufacturing where it hurt, in its north and Midlands heartlands. Not only did service industries escape lightly from that recession, but subsequent policies encouraged them. The easy-money environment of the 1980s, the removal of controls on consumer credit and tax cuts, provided the basis for a long, consumer-driven upturn and gave a boost to retailing. At the same time, financial liberalisation provided the basis for big expansion in banking, insurance and finance. The south in general, and the southeast in particular, cleaned up.

Between 1985 and 1989, for example, unemployment averaged 6.6% of the workforce in the southeast and East Anglia, 11.9% in the northwest and 13.4% in the northeast. House prices in London and the southeast, at the peak of the divide, were $2\frac{1}{2}$ times those in Yorkshire and Humberside.

Then, or course, came the 1990–92 "white-collar" recession, the scourge of negative equity – which hit heavily-mortgaged southerners hardest – and a levelling out of regional differences in unemployment. By 1993, for example, unemployment in the southeast, at more than 10%, was higher than in Scotland or Wales, similar to Yorkshire and Humberside, and just below the northwest. The north–south divide was dead, people said.

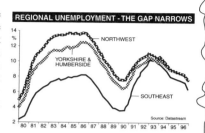

REGIONAL UNEMPLOYMENT - THE GAP NARROWS

Now, however, there are signs it may have been merely sleeping. The European Commission, in its "cohesion report" on regional differences within Europe, published late last year, said Britain was still suffering from an economic divide between the prosperous south and the poorer north.

Business Strategies, the consultancy headed by Bridget Rosewell, the Treasury "wise woman", says half the 1.6m new jobs created over the next decade will be in London and the southeast, while the northeast will have a net fall in employment and the northwest only a tiny rise. To the extent that sterling's strength steers activity away from manufacturing to services, this effect will be exaggerated.

David Kern, NatWest's chief economist, says some of this is already happening, with employment having grown by 3.9%, on average, in southern regions during this growth period, compared with only 1.4% in the north.

David Smith

Sunday Times, 5 January 1997

As indicated in Figure 2 on page 11, the level of long-term unemployment was much higher at the start of the 1990s than at the beginning of the previous recession. If the short-run NAIRU did not increase as a result, this may reflect the success of employment policies, such as Restart, introduced in 1986 (see Chapter 4). It seems that in the 1990s, a fall in **search effectiveness** as the length of unemployment increases is less of a problem than it had been in much of the 1980s.

So, there is some evidence of success for supply side policies directed at search effectiveness. Unfortunately, it is not clear that the same can be said of **training policies.** The quality of training available to the unemployed through Training for Work and through Employment Training, which preceded it, is low. The employment rate of those completing government training schemes is disappointing. *It seems that the training the unemployed receive is doing little to tackle the mismatch created by the change in the skills required of the labour force.* At a time when unemployment is still unacceptably high, microeconomic policies designed to increase the economy's capacity to supply without generating inflation have much to recommend them.

KEY WORDS

Base rate
Exchange rate mechanism
Overheating

Search effectiveness
Training policies

Reading list
Smith, D., *UK Current Economic Policy*, Heinemann Educational, 1994.

Essay Topics
1. (a) What is meant by the 'natural rate of unemployment'? [20 marks]
   (b) Examine how the natural rate of unemployment might be reduced. [40 marks]
   (c) Analyse the likely consequences of attempting to reduce unemployment below its natural rate. [40 marks]
   [University of London Examinations and Assessment Council 1993]
2. (a) Explain the economic costs which result from unemployment. [12 marks]

(b) Discuss the various factors which have caused the fluctuations in unemployment in the United Kingdom during the past decade. [13 marks]
[Associated Examining Board 1995]

3 'Whitehall plans for 2.5 million jobless through the 1990s.' (Headline in *The Independent*, 9 December 1991). What constrains the ability of the UK government to reduce unemployment? [20 marks]
[University of Oxford Delegacy of Local Examinations 1993]

Data Response Question
Earnings and inflation in the UK economy

This task is based on a question set by the University of Cambridge Local Examinations Syndicate in 1995. Look at the table and read the article by John Philpott then answer the questions.

Table 1 gives an analysis of the distribution of earnings. The median refers to the mid-point of the distribution and the data are expressed as a percentage of the median pay of men and women for 1979 and 1993. In 1993 median earnings were £304.60 for men and £221.60 for women. Therefore, from the table, in 1993 90% of men earned more than 57% of the median wage for men, i.e. more than £173.62.

Table 1 Distribution of earnings as a percentage of median pay

	Men		Women	
	1979 % of median pay	1993 % of median pay	1979 % of median pay	1993 % of median pay
top 10% earned more than	157	186	159	181
top 25% earned more than	125	137	125	140
top 50% earned more than	100	100	100	100
top 75% earned more than	80	74	82	76
top 90% earned more than	66	57	69	61

Notes: the figures relate to gross weekly earnings of full-time adult employees whose pay was not affected by absence in April each year.
Source: Department of Employment *New Earnings Survey*, 1993, Part A, HMSO

Wages Councils Abolished

The Trade Union Reform and Employment Rights Act 1993 brought to an end the 84-year-old system of legal minimum wages. Until that date it was the role of the Wages Councils to determine them. At abolition the 26 Wages Councils determined minimum rates of pay for 2.4 million workers, mostly non-union women working in the service sector – in shops, restaurants, hairdressers etc. – but also some parts of manufacturing.

The Wages Councils did little to raise the relative pay of the low-paid, but they may have prevented it from falling. The government's precise reason for abolishing the councils was unclear. Ministers have sometimes implied that minimum wages priced unskilled workers out of jobs and led to higher unemployment. In defending abolition of the councils, however, former Employment Secretary Gillian Shephard argued that they were irrelevant, since most workers covered by the councils' Wages Orders earned more than the minimum rates of pay being set.

If the latter claim proved true, abolition would have little effect other than to save the money spent on the councils' administrative machinery. If the councils did serve to price some workers out of jobs, however, reform should lead to more jobs – but with the consequence of even lower pay for some of the weakest groups in the labour market.

Source: adapted from 'The Labour Market' by John Philpott in *Focus on Britain 1994* edited by Philip Allan, John Benyon and Barry McCormick published by Perennial Publications, 1994

---

1. Give **two** reasons to explain the differences in the median pay of men and women in 1993. [4 marks]
2. Use a supply and demand diagram to explain
   (a) why 'minimum wages priced unskilled workers out of jobs'. [3 marks]
   (b) the statement that 'the councils were irrelevant since most workers covered by the councils' Wages Orders earned more than the minimum rates of pay being set'. [3 marks]
3. (a) What evidence is there to support the view that, for employees as a whole, the pay gap (i.e. the gap between the highest and lowest paid) has widened between 1979 and 1993? [2 marks]
   (b) Explain why the pay gap has widened. [4 marks]
4. Discuss the likely impact of the abolition of the Wages Councils on the pay gap for women. [4 marks]

Chapter Six

International comparisons

*'The evidence is that slow productivity growth does not relieve unem-
ployment nor does rapid productivity growth exacerbate it.'*
McKinsey Global Institute

As Chapters 1, 2, 4 and 5 have demonstrated, the UK has experienced
a number of striking variations in its unemployment rate over the past
25 years. Is the UK unique in this respect, or have other industrialized
countries undergone the same experience? We should expect some
similarities since a number of economic shocks hit such countries at
the same time. However, in the long run, these similarities disappear
because policy responses differ widely between countries.

Figure 1 showed that there are some similarities between the UK's
and the USA's unemployment performance: both experienced sharp
rises after the oil price shocks of 1974 and 1979, and both posted falls
in the mid-80s and rises in the late 1980s. However, there are probably
as many differences as similarities. From 1960 until 1968, US unemployment fell, while that of the UK rose. More remarkably, for every
year up until 1980, the US unemployment rate was higher than that of
the UK; for every year since 1980 the opposite has been true. The gap
has been as large as $3\frac{1}{2}$ percentage points in 1984 and is still currently
around 3 percentage points. Japan's unemployment performance can
be seen in Figure 10 on page 24. Although there has been a slight
upward trend in recent years, its unemployment rate is lower than that
of almost any other OECD country, and has been much lower than
that of the UK ever since the first oil-price shock. In the past three
years the US unemployment rate has not been above 6 per cent, and
that in Japan has not been above 4 per cent in the past thirty. By way
of contrast, the unemployment rate in the United Kingdom has only
been below 6 per cent once in the past sixteen years, in 1990.

Since 1980, the UK's unemployment performance has thus been less
good than that of both the US and Japan. However, some might say
that this is too select a comparison group and that we should also
analyse the UK's performance relative to a group of similar countries.
Figures 19 and 20 thus summarize unemployment and inflation rates
in the UK and two mutually exclusive groups of countries: the fifteen
countries of the European Union minus the UK (this group will be

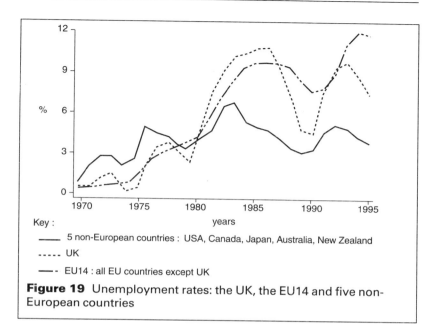

Figure 19 Unemployment rates: the UK, the EU14 and five non-European countries

referred to as the EU14), and a group of five non-European industrialized countries (the USA, Canada, Japan, Australia and New Zealand). All figures for these groups refer to weighted averages.

Figure 19 shows that the rise in unemployment which has hit the UK has also been experienced by EU and, to a lesser extent, the group of five countries. There has been a noticeable reversal of ordering: up until 1979, the non-European countries had the highest unemployment rate; from 1981 onwards, they have had the lowest. UK unemployment has moved to some extent in the same way as that of the other countries in the European Union. From 1981 until 1987, UK unemployment was higher than that in other EU countries, and four years then followed during which it was lower. After rising back up to EU levels in 1992, UK unemployment now stands some $3\frac{1}{2}$ percentage points lower than in the EU14. But UK unemployment is still 3 percentage points higher than the unemployment rate in the non-European countries. Part of the explanation for the UK's better unemployment performance than the rest of the EU undoubtedly lies in the different stages of the economic cycle at which different countries find themselves. Among the other EU countries, there are those in recession (France, Belgium, Germany and Sweden), as well as those with unemployment rates below that of the UK (Denmark, the Netherlands and Portugal).

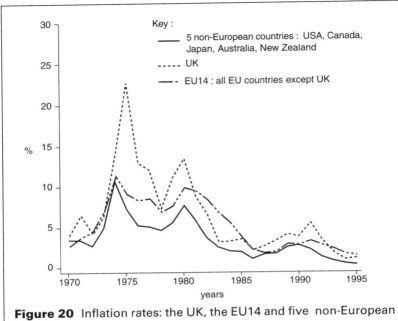

Figure 20 Inflation rates: the UK, the EU14 and five non-European countries

Following on from the theory outlined in Chapter 3, we might wonder whether the difference in unemployment performance in Figure 19 is reflected in inflation rates. Figure 20 shows that the overriding tendency over the past fifteen years has been for inflation to fall, down to current levels of around 3 per cent. UK inflation is higher than that of the five non-European countries for every year in the graph; it is also higher than average inflation in the other EU countries, with the exception of 1973, the recessionary period of 1981–85, and the three most recent years graphed (where the difference is only very small).

These two measures of performance may be combined into a **misery index**. This is defined as the sum of the inflation and unemployment rates, and it is graphed in Figure 21.

The three misery indices share some common features, moving upwards and peaking at the time of the first oil-price shock, peaking again for the second oil-price shock, and then (mostly) falling from the early 1980s onwards. However, it is interesting to note that the three indices were almost identical until 1974, but that from then on there has been a growing split between European and non-European performance: the misery index of the latter group of countries is currently back to below its early-1970s level, while that of the EU countries

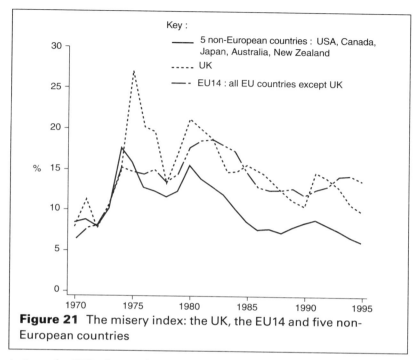

Figure 21 The misery index: the UK, the EU14 and five non-European countries

(minus the UK), despite having fallen from its 1980s peak, is still twice as high as it was before the oil-price shocks.

The UK's performance moves around a lot more than does that for the EU14 (which is unsurprising as the latter is an average across quite a lot of different countries). The UK misery index hit a much higher peak than that of either the EU14 or the non-European countries after 1974, largely because of its much worse inflation performance (see Figure 20). The UK's index remained higher than the two others until 1982, when it dropped below that of the EU14. There then followed a number of cycles. The UK performed better than the EU14 (at least as far as this simple index measures) for only three years, then performs worse, also for three years, then again better, from 1988 to 1990 (you guessed, three years), and worse again in 1991 and 1992. The UK's misery index is currently halfway between that of the non-European countries and that of the EU14. Given the experience of the past fifteen years, the key question is whether such a position is tenable. The recent downwards trend in unemployment has revived fears of higher inflation. In terms of the model of Chapter 3, if unemployment is less than the NAIRU then (sooner or later) inflation will rise. That seems to have been the history of the last 20 years, and the fact that there is

ECONOMIC COMPETITIVENESS

It hurt, but did it work?

After 17 years of painful Tory reforms, does Britain's economy now hold its own against the best of its international rivals, or is it still falling behind? This will be hotly debated in the general election. Both main political parties are already on the attack. The government is boasting about last week's glowing report from the OECD and a competitiveness league table that put Britain above the big continental European economies.

...Labour, meanwhile, took Britain's poor showing in another competitiveness ranking published last week as more proof of economic decline under the Tories. It has been claiming *ad nauseam* that between 1979 and 1994 Britain fell from 13th to 18th in the "world prosperity league table". Who is right?

League tables of economic competitiveness should always be taken with several pinches of salt, not least because economists are split over what, if anything, competitiveness means. Last week's pair of rankings reflects this uncertainty. Each relied on scores of different measures, some quantitative, others qualitative; Britain was ranked differently because the measures used were different. But even the apparently authoritative "prosperity league" quoted by Labour, ranking countries by GDP per head, reveals less than it first appears to do.

...But arguments about exact rankings probably mislead by suggesting precision. In order to make comparisons, each country's GDP is adjusted to ensure "purchasing power parity" – that is, using the exchange rate which makes the price of goods and services the same in every country. This is more art than science, and a wide margin for error should be applied to any figure, points out Martin Weale, director of the National Institute of Economic and Social Research (NIESR). The differences in GDP per head for those countries between Japan in 7th place and Sweden in 20th are too small for the rankings to be reliable. What is clear, though, is that Britain is no longer falling behind the pack.

...A similar story is revealed by looking beneath the headline GDP numbers. Start with the labour market, which the Tories regard as one of their greatest successes. Overall, Britain's labour productivity has improved. According to Richard Layard, an economist at the London School of Economics, between 1973 and 1994 it grew at an annual rate of 1.2%, half the EU average. Between 1979 and 1994 it grew at an average of 1.9% a year. That is faster than in France, Germany and America, although slower than in Japan. However, the differences between countries are mostly tiny compared with the 1970s, says Mr Layard, and Britain's performance is again best described as rejoining the pack. Labour productivity grew most in manufacturing where it made up much of the shortfall compared with productivity in Japan and Germany in 1979. Overall though, the record is not outstanding.

The Economist, 8 June 1996

currently some evidence of increasing inflation suggests that unemployment has now fallen too far to be consistent with stable inflation, and that the misery index might bounce back up again towards European levels unless action is taken to reduce the NAIRU.

The experience of the last few years has shown something more of a convergence in unemployment rates across industrialized countries, with the early 1990s seeing post-war record unemployment rates in Western Europe, in the Scandinavian Countries and in Oceania. But even in this period of convergence, individual countries, such as the USA, Japan, (recently) New Zealand and Denmark, have outperformed others. Figure 21 above shows that, on average, the UK seems to have done about as well as Europe. But the key point is that Europe has performed terribly over the past 20 years, whereas other countries, and other groups of countries, have done better. The lesson to be learned from international comparisons is again that no country should be fated to endure high unemployment.

KEY WORDS

Misery index

Essay topics

1. (a) Explain how supply side policies might be used to: (i) reduce the level of unemployment; (ii) increase the rate of economic growth. [70 marks]

   (b) To what extent have supply side policies been effective in achieving these aims in the UK? [30 marks]

   [University of London Examinations and Assessment Council 1996]

2. Would an increase in government expenditure or in private sector investment be more effective in reducing United Kingdom unemployment? [20 marks]

   [University of Oxford Delegacy of Local Examinations 1994]

Data Response Question

Unemployment in Europe

This task is based on a question set by the University of London Examinations and Assessment Council in 1996. Read the article and answer the questions.

1. What is the distinction between structural and cyclical unemployment? [2 marks]

2. Why has Germany played a key role in European interest rate determination? [3 marks]
3. What is meant by 'a flexible market for labour'? [2 marks]
4. Explain, with the aid of a diagram, the argument that 'France's high rate of unemployment among the young is partly due to the national minimum wage at nearly 50% of average earnings'. [4 marks]
5. Other than the policies mentioned in the passage, what supply side measures could governments use to reduce the level of unemployment? [5 marks]
6. What might be the economic impact of 'raising import barriers against suppliers in Eastern Europe and developing countries'? [4 marks]

Business is booming for suppliers of bad ideas on how to cut unemployment. A careful appraisal of which anti-unemployment measures to adopt, and which to avoid, is still needed. In the present debate, there are three main groups: those who argue that the European Community's [now the EU] unemployment is cyclical, implying that the cure is to ease monetary policy; those who see the problem as mainly structural, and conclude that improved competitiveness by itself is the cure; and those who agree that the unemployment is structural, but would rather raise import barriers against suppliers in Eastern Europe and developing countries.

All three groups are dangerously in error. For a start, Europe's unemployment is plainly neither cyclical nor structural, but a mixture of both. Its cyclical part is largely due to Germany, whose policies have obliged other members of the ERM to keep interest rates higher than they would wish.

Those who are keen on faster growth think monetary policy is, therefore, too tight. But unemployment in the Community has averaged 9.9% of the labour force for the past ten years; even at the most recent peak in economic activity the rate was 9.3%. Given such figures, it is clear that a large part of the EC's unemployment problem is deep-seated and non-cyclical. Something more imaginative than pumping up aggregate demand is needed to deal with it.

What exactly? Improved competitiveness, desirable as that is, will not be enough. Low unemployment requires a flexible market for labour. Often, that goes hand in hand with greater competitiveness, and policies to further the one will tend to help the other. You also need a labour market that works, one that moves workers displaced from contracting industries into new jobs in expanding ones.

A chief cause – especially of the rising toll of long-term unemployment – is welfare benefits that are too generous for too long, and which place too few demands on recipients to find a new job.

A government must avoid doing things that make unemployment worse. There is little doubt, for instance, that France's high rate of unemployment among the young is partly due to the national minimum wage – at nearly 50% of average earnings (covering roughly 12% of wage-earners).

Greater competitiveness (unlike new trade barriers) would make the EC richer. Policies to foster it are certainly desirable. But on their own they will not cure Europe's unemployment sickness.

Source: 'Jobless Europe', *The Economist*, 26 June 1993

Chapter Seven
Myths about unemployment

'... This argument is like the voice of the siren; it sounds sweet and reasonable, but it leads to disaster.' Richard Layard

Chapters 4 and 5 outlined our theory of why unemployment in the UK has been so high during the 1980s and 1990s. Before we move on to consider various proposals for dealing with the problem, we shall analyse some rival explanations of high UK unemployment.

Myth 1: More technological unemployment

This first myth is widespread. Very many people believe that the rise in unemployment is due to modern technology, and for this reason they are deeply pessimistic about whether we could ever have full employment again. It is certainly true that machines are constantly replacing people, in task after task. But this cannot be why unemployment has increased so much recently. If changes of that kind caused higher unemployment, then unemployment would have been rising since the Industrial Revolution. There have been great **productivity** breakthroughs in the past, but these have not led to prolonged general unemployment. We had the steam engine, revolutions in spinning and weaving, the electric motor, the sewing machine, the internal combustion engine, the jet engine, and the plastics revolution. Particular workers often lost their jobs, but there was no general tendency to rising unemployment.

When **technical change** actually happens, there are of course changes in employment. Sometimes it goes up (as in the high-tech industries), sometimes it goes down (as with containerization in the docks). Either way, there is some dislocation while new patterns of employment are established. But there is no evidence that high productivity growth has normally been a long-lasting source of difficulty. In the UK, productivity growth was unusually high in the 1950s and 1960s, as in much of the 1980s. But in the 1950s and 1960s, it caused no unemployment. It was when productivity growth fell in the 1970s that unemployment became a problem, owing to the difficulties of satisfying the demand for higher real wages and living standards. In other words the fall in productivity growth led to a gap between the feasible and the target real wages. In fact, the major country with the lowest unemployment

Technology and unemployment

Since the beginning of the industrial revolution people have predicted that machines would destroy jobs. In the early 19th century the Luddites responded by destroying the looms and jennies that threatened their livelihood. Marx said that, by investing in machinery, factory owners would create a vast army of unemployed. And in the late 1940s Norbert Weiner, a pioneer of computing, forecast that this new technology would destroy enough jobs to make the depression of the 1930s look like a picnic.

Fear of what machines will do to men at work waxes and wanes. Right now, the fear is growing strongly. Typical of the new wave of pessimistic forecasts is a book, "The End of Work" (G.P. Putnam's Sons), by Jeremy Rifkin, an American technophobe whose previous target was the biotechnology industry. Within the next century, he predicts, the world's rich economies will have virtually no need of workers. Predictions such as this reinforce a growing fear in the middle classes that technology, having eliminated much of the work previously done by manual workers, is about to cut a swathe through white-collar ranks as well.

Are such fears justified? In one way, yes. Millions of jobs have indeed been destroyed by technology. A decade ago, the words you are now reading would have reached you from two sets of hands: those of a journalist and those of a typesetter. Thanks to computers, the typesetter no longer has a job. But cheer up – a bit, anyway. Although the typesetter no longer has that job, he may well have a different one. John Kennedy put it well in the 1960s: "If men have the talent to invent new machines that put men out of work, they have the talent to put those men back to work." That is as true now as it was then, and earlier.

In the past 200 years millions of manual workers have been replaced by machines. Over the same period, the number of jobs has grown almost continuously, as have the real incomes of most people in the industrial world. Furthermore, this growth and enrichment have come about not in spite of techonological change but because of it.

The idea that technology is capable of creating more jobs than it destroys, and will do so again, would not surprise an economist.

A new machine helps you make more stuff with fewer people. But the assumption that this results in fewer jobs rather than more output (and hence more goods, and more job-stimulating demand, in a beautifully virtuous circle) is based on an economic fallacy known as the "lump of labour": the notion that there is only a fixed amount of output (and hence work) to go round. This is clearly wrong. Technology creates new demand, either by increasing productivity and hence real incomes, or by creating new goods.

The Economist, 11 February 1995

is the one with the highest productivity growth: Japan.

But surely, you might say, high labour productivity (i.e. high output per worker) must be bad for employment in the economy. For if output does not rise but output per worker does, fewer workers are needed. But why assume that output does not rise? When it becomes possible to produce more output, the normal result is that more output *is* produced. This is what has happened over the centuries. The problem today is that output is low in relation to what could be produced, not that the people who do have jobs are producing too much.

The most basic fallacy in economics is the 'lump of output' fallacy: to take output as given. So let us ask instead why the actual output of the economy is lower than it could be. Some people say it is because of satiation – i.e. people now have all they need. That view is an insult to all those who live in shabby houses with ill-fed children. There may be some Hampstead trendies or busy stockbrokers for whom extra cash would do no good, but to talk of satiation in general is immoral. The fact is that output is low not because people do not want more, and not because it couldn't be higher, but rather because any policy that increases demand for the economy's output would be unsustainable in that it would lead to accelerating inflation.

Myth 2: Too many people

Many people think that unemployment is high because of the increase in the **labour force** (due to immigration, for example). This is most unlikely. In the nineteenth century, the labour force grew much faster than it has recently, with no increase in unemployment. Even in the period 1950–65, the labour force grew as fast as in the 1980s, and we now think of the former period as representing a 'golden age' for low unemployment.

In the short run, various factors may influence the labour force and thus lead to changes in unemployment. For example, it could be argued that unemployment in the 1980s was exacerbated by two distinct factors. The first was the **demographic** influence of many more young people coming on to the job market as one of the 'baby boom' generations started to turn sixteen. The other was the increased tendency of women to enter the labour force. Between 1981 and 1989, the **participation rate** of women in the UK – *that is the percentage of women of working age either working or unemployed* – rose from 47.6 to 53 per cent. This activity rate, which is currently 54 per cent, is projected to carry on rising, leading to a larger labour force. This rise, however, will be offset by a 'baby bust' as the number of school-leavers entering the labour market falls. Births in the UK reached a low in 1978, meaning that there are relatively fewer people 'coming on stream' in the labour market between 1994 and 1999.

The effects of the labour force on unemployment are short-term: the number of people is not a major factor in the long run. This is confirmed by looking at other countries. As Figure 10 on page 22 showed, there has been a huge rise in the labour force in both the USA and Japan, but with no great change in unemployment. In the USA, both the labour force and employment have risen by about 80 per cent in the last 30 years. The fact is that a normally functioning economy will find jobs for all the people around who want them.

Myth 3: Unemployment would be lower if work were shared out more equally

This is another commonly held view. It states that if everyone were to work shorter hours, or share jobs, or retire earlier, then we could benefit from an immediate reduction in the numbers unemployed.

Let us consider the case for shorter **working hours** per week (the other cases can be analysed similarly). Suppose that the economy is going to produce a certain level of output, so that there are, roughly speaking, a certain total number of hours to be worked each week. If there are people unemployed, then it would be better to reduce the hours worked by each worker and increase the number of workers. This would allocate work more fairly and it would reduce unemployment.

This argument seems plausible if we think of reducing hours at just one workplace. Yet, if all workplaces reduce hours at the same time, the argument only works on a critical assumption which is often ignored, namely that output remains constant – the 'lump of output' proposition. From the analysis in Chapter 3, we remember that, if the NAIRU stays the same, then whenever unemployment falls, inflation rises more, or falls less, than it would have done otherwise. So, using shorter working hours to cut unemployment leads to a rise in the rate of inflation over what would have occurred otherwise.

Two responses are then possible. First, the government could accept the rising inflation. But if it were to do this, then it would obviously have been better to cut unemployment by expanding output rather than by redistributing the current amount of work. Second, the government could decide that rising inflation is unacceptable and thus allow unemployment to rise to its former level. The shorter working hours will then have had no final effect on unemployment, but will have decreased output.

There seems, then, to be little theoretical use for arguing that shorter working hours (or **early retirement** or **job sharing**) present a valid case for reducing unemployment. And the evidence over the past fifteen years from a number of different countries shows that shorter working hours seem to be associated with greater rather than smaller rises in unemployment. A very similar picture can be drawn for the increase in early retirement and the increase in unemployment. Both theory and facts thus seem to tell against this myth.

KEY WORDS

Technological unemployment
Productivity
Technical change
Labour force
Demography

Participation rate
Working hours
Early retirement
Job sharing

Reading list
Simpson, L., and Paterson, I., *The UK Labour Market*, Heinemann Educational, 1995.

Essay topics
1. Explain and discuss the following:

   (a) part-time workers often being paid at an hourly rate less than full-time workers [8 marks]

   (b) firms paying overtime rates that are greater than normal wage rates [8 marks]

   (c) government subsidizing employers who take on additional workers from those who have been unemployed for at least six months. [9 marks]

   [University of Oxford Delegacy of Local Examinations 1995]

2. How does the analysis and classification of unemployment contribute to our understanding of how to deal with it? Compare government training schemes, increases in aggregate demand and cuts in real wages as ways of dealing with unemployment. [25 marks]

   [Northern Examination and Assessment Board 1993]

Data Response Question

Productivity and pay
This task is based on a question set by the Joint Matriculation Board in 1991. Study Table A and the two articles from the *Times* and the *Financial Times*, then answer the following questions.

1. Outline the arguments, as presented in the articles, for and against linking productivity and pay.
2. In the light of economic theory, how would you expect the relationship between productivity and pay to affect the level of employment and the degree of inflation in the economy? What support, if any, for your ideas do you find in Table A?
3. Is it possible to establish principles to ensure that payment to service sector employees is fair and efficient?

Table A UK manufacturing industry (1985 = 100)

	Employed labour force	Output per person employed	Average weekly earnings per head	Index of retail prices
1982	107.0	84.7	77.4	85.9
1983	102.1	91.8	84.4	89.8
1984	100.5	97.1	91.7	94.3
1985	100.0	100.0	100.0	100.0
1986	97.9	103.1	107.7	103.4
1987	97.0	109.9	116.3	107.7
1988	98.5	115.9	126.2	113.0
1989	98.5	121.6	137.2	121.8

Sources: CSO *Economic Trends,* July 1990; *Employment Gazette,* March 1990

No return to a going rate

John Banham

The recent discussion of pay awards has a depressingly familiar ring. Ford is said to be setting a 'going rate' of over 10 per cent which will be followed by others, not only in manufacturing. 'Pay explosion,' scream the headlines. Ministers urge restraint and warn of the consequences of irresponsibility.

For the best part of 30 years successive governments sought to cajole employers towards a set figure for annual pay rises regardless of whether they had been earned or not. The result was a low-pay, low-productivity economy slipping inexorably down the league table of international competitiveness. The norm became an entitlement.

Only since the trading sector broke free of the going-rate mentality have we started to regain international competitiveness. Employers are constantly balancing the need to pay no more – and no less – than is required to attract and keep the necessary skills and commitment against the need to remain cost-competitive.

With the price of manufactured goods in the shops rising by around 4 per cent per year, it is clear that such a balance can be achieved only with improved performance. Since 1980, manufacturing productivity in Britain has risen by some 60 per cent overall, though with widely varying performances. The CBI's Pay Databank shows that employers expect to achieve further substantial improvement, on average of about 6 per cent, this year.

CBI data show that during the first half of the 1980s at least two-thirds of all firms linked pay to productivity, and the trend has continued since. Employment has risen to record levels, and, according to a recent consumer survey, there has been a perceived improvement in the quality of British-made goods. Export revenues (excluding oil) have been particularly buoyant: Britain's share of world manufactured exports is now rising, probably for the first time this century. It is not generally recognized that we export more, per head of population, than Japan.

All this shows what can be achieved when employers are free to build pay structures that suit their circumstances, and to pursue wage settlements that are financed by real improvements in performance. And at least one manufacturer in three is still achieving productivity improvements that outstrip the corresponding pay settlements.

To say this is not to under-estimate the difficulties of maintaining progress towards an internationally competitive manufacturing base, which holds the key to redressing our balance of payments deficit and curbing inflation. With poorer prospects for growth in the domestic market, manufacturers are having to redouble their export efforts to cover investment costs under a high interest rate regime. Since mid-1988, when interest rates took off, employers have also been grappling with inflationary pressures on pay.

Despite the improvement, the link between pay and performance is still not strong enough to ensure that in all cases unit labour costs fall year by year, as they must in a competitive world. If they do not, the result will be fewer jobs. That is why the CBI emphasizes that pay rises must always be linked to improved productivity. There can be only one going rate. It is for unit labour costs. And our international competitors have ensured that it must be negative.

Source: *The Times*, 18 January 1990

The fallacy about productivity and pay

RICHARD LAYARD

Should workers be paid according to the productivity of their enterprise? According to senior ministers and CBI leaders the answer is Yes. But the standard answer has always been No.

So where do ministers go wrong? They start from the important proposition that to stop inflation, average wages in the economy should rise only as fast as average productivity. They then suppose that an easy way to achieve this would be if pay in each firm grew at the same rate as productivity in the same firm.

But this method is disastrous and doomed to failure. It is not only unfair but grossly inefficient. There are huge differences in productivity growth between sectors, which are mainly due to technological factors and not to the efforts of the workers. Thus some sectors have inherently greater productivity growth than others – with manufacturing generally outstripping services. Since this reflects no special merit among the workers in manufacturing, why should workers in services increasingly fall behind?

The service workers will not, of course, agree to do so, and market forces are on their side. So the chief result will be additional inflationary pressure, as service workers' pay tries to keep pace with manufacturing. This is the fundamental problem behind the ambulance workers' dispute.

The mechanism can be simply illustrated. Suppose productivity grows at 5 per cent a year in 'manufacturing' and 1 per cent in 'services' – an average of, say, 3 per cent. If all workers get 3 per cent wage increases, all will be well. But that is not the current philosophy. Government ministers have told those in 'manufacturing' that they can reasonably expect more. But then the 'service' workers also insist on getting more too. The result is disastrous.

An important reason for our present problems is this half-baked philosophy. Yet these issues are not new. In 1967 William Baumol wrote a famous article in which he explained how economic progress proceeds in a properly functioning economy. Productivity grows faster in manufacturing than in services. But wages grow at the same rate (so that the relative price of manufactures falls).

In this way the fruits of high productivity growth are spread evenly across the economy, not hogged by one group of workers. Thus barbers are four times richer than they were half a century ago because of productivity increases in the rest of the economy. How on earth could anybody believe that efficiency or equity required otherwise?

The inefficiency in productivity-based pay is manifest. If firms with high productivity growth pay higher wages, rather than cutting their prices, their sales will be depressed. Employment in the most productive sectors will be held back, and the least productive sectors (paying lower wages) will continue to waste labour. In international competition the country will be increasingly forced to specialise in low-productivity, low-wage industries.

This is the opposite of what would happen in a proper competitive labour market. Under competition, workers of a given type would be paid the same regardless of who employed them. And this would ensure that as a nation we best exploited our international comparative advantage.

Source: *Financial Times,* 31 January 1990

Chapter Eight

Remedies: The debate

'Few people at Westminster retain much faith in remedies at a macro-economic level.' The Economist, June 1992

What can be done about unemployment? As we argued in Chapter 4, unemployment is determined by supply factors in the medium term and by demand factors in the short term. Increased demand for labour lowers unemployment, but without supply side measures, the medium- and long-term effect is likely to be higher inflation rather than lower unemployment. The debate on the remedies for unemployment centres on what, if any, supply side measures should be taken to lower the NAIRU and how effective they would be.

First, **targeting** the increased demand to bring the most benefit to jobs might stop it from spilling over into higher wages and prices. The aim of targeting is to concentrate the extra demand on slack parts of the economy. Successful targeting not only does the least inflationary damage but also improves the supply capacity of the economy by making more use of existing resources.

Many of the suggested remedies for unemployment involve targeting assistance on the **long-term unemployed.** Long-term unemployment, as already mentioned, is unemployment which has lasted more than one year. In Chapter 2, we set out some basic facts about long-term unemployment. In Chapter 3, we showed how high long-term unemployment led to a short-run NAIRU above the long-run NAIRU. *Most long-term unemployed people are so discouraged and stigmatized that employers simply do not see them as part of the effective supply of labour.* Figure 22 demonstrates just how much being unemployed for a long time reduces the chance of finding a job.

This figure shows that over half of men who became unemployed in 1994 stopped claiming benefit within three months of signing on. The vast majority of these had found work. Almost nine out of ten men who had been unemployed for more than four years in 1994 continued to claim benefit for at least another three months. Even among the small minority of the very long-term unemployed who signed off benefit, many had not found work; some, for example, claimed sickness or invalidity benefit instead of benefit for unemployment. Following the introduction of incapacity benefit in 1995, it may now be harder for the long-term unemployed to withdraw from the labour market in this way.

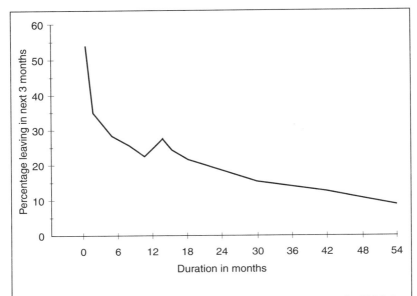

Figure 22 Unemployed men leaving the claimant count in 1994, by duration of unemployment

With this extra information on the long-term unemployed, we can now set out a number of proposed remedies for unemployment in more detail and consider some objections to them. In addition to targeting demand, three supply side remedies are widely advocated:

- changes to the social security system, often summed up by the slogan **'from welfare to work'**
- **raising skills**
- limiting inflationary pressures directly through a **national economic assessment.**

Remedy 1: Targeting demand
Targeting directs increased public spending (as far as possible) towards unemployed people and people at high risk of unemployment – the young, those in high-unemployment areas, and semi-skilled and unskilled workers. For example, the government could give money to local economic initiatives in areas of very high unemployment, such as those highlighted on pages 21–2. The government could also require employers working on major publicly financed projects, such as road building, to employ some long-term unemployed people.

Reducing the cost of labour in high-unemployment regions through lower employers' **National Insurance contributions** is another way of targeting demand. The problem here is that the effect of lower employers' contributions on labour costs is unclear. If market forces determine labour costs, wages in high-unemployment regions would rise. As a result lower contributions might have no effect on labour demand, employment or unemployment. Still, reducing labour costs seems more likely to affect regional unemployment than does reducing the cost of capital – as regional policy does at present.

A more radical idea is to use employers' National Insurance contributions to shift labour demand from more-skilled to less-skilled employees. The relative demand for less-skilled people has fallen sharply in the 1980s and 1990s. The skills of the labour force have improved but not enough to prevent increasing mismatch. So, increasing employers' National Insurance contributions for the highly paid and reducing their contributions for the low-paid should lessen mismatch and thus unemployment.

Remedy 2: From welfare to work

A very different solution to the excess supply of less-skilled workers (relative to demand) has been tried in the early 1990s. Market forces have been allowed to push the wages of the less-skilled down (at least relative to average earnings), and benefits have targeted on the low-paid via means testing. Between 1991 and 1996, government spending on in-work benefits, such as **Family Credit,** grew by 14 per cent a year, after allowing for inflation. A major reason for the growth in in-work benefits is to increase incentives for the employed to take low-paid work. The companion volume *Welfare State Economics,* gives more details on the effect of benefits on work incentives.

The 'from welfare to work' remedy emphasizes active labour market policy, which we considered in Chapter 4. It involves an ambitious package of policies, which we list in order of probable cost-effectiveness – those that research suggests have the greatest effect on unemployment relative to their cost coming first:

- **job-search measures**
- **recruitment subsidies**
- **adult training.**

Job-search measures include counselling, job placement assistance, training and practical help in seeking work, and stricter requirements for benefit claimants to 'actively seek work'. These job-search measures have the advantage of reaching large numbers of the unemployed at low cost,. Low cost, rather than a big effect on unemployment, is the main reason for job-search measures being top of the list in terms of cost-effectiveness. Still, there is evidence that Restart interviews, when first introduced in 1986, reduced long-term unemployment by up to 10 per cent.

Recruitment subsidies aim to get the unemployed straight into regular jobs by giving money to employers who recruit the unemployed. Subsidies can be targeted by limiting them to the long-term unemployed. Disadvantanges of recruitment subsidies include:

- **Deadweight costs,** *that is the costs of recruitment subsidies given to those employers who would have recruited the same unemployed people without subsidy.*

No free lunch for the jobless

Instead of paying the unemployed to stay at home, why not pay the same money as a subsidy to encourage firms to hire them?

The idea that governments should subsidise the wages of jobless workers has often been floated as a near-painless way to reduce unemployment. The theory is attractive. Instead of receiving welfare benefits, unemployed workers would get a voucher promising that the state would pay part of their wage if they found a job. This would reduce the cost of labour and so encourage employers to hire extra workers. And it would cost the government nothing: the cost of subsidies would be met by savings in benefits.

If only life were that simple. Two decades of trials in several countries have produced disappointing results, with only a small net increase in jobs. Wage-subsidy schemes have proved leaky in at least three significant ways:

- **Deadweight costs.** Some workers would have found jobs even without a subsidy. Needlessly subsidising workers produces what are known as dead-weight costs. Studies suggest that two-thirds of participants in early schemes in Australia and Ireland would have got their jobs without any subsidy.
- **Displacement.** At worst, a wage subsidy could be so tempting that employers fired existing workers in order to hire subsidised ones. But even at best, vouchers might benefit participants by harming the prospects for other jobseekers who do not qualify for subsidies. Three-quarters of the workers helped by a Dutch scheme were found to have filled vacancies at the expense of other jobless workers.
- **Short-termism.** Subsidies cannot and should not last forever. There is therefore a risk that employers will dump workers once the subsidy runs out (as many American bosses did in one trial).

A review of studies by the OECD suggests that deadweight costs and displacement often account for 80–90% of the participation in wage-subsidy schemes.

The Economist, 20 August 1994

- **Displacement,** *that is employers, recruiting people who are subsidized instead of people who are not subsidized.* In other words, people who are subsidized displace from employment those who are not.
- **Short-termism.** Recruitment subsidies only last for a short period. *When the subsidies end, the employment they have subsidized may also end.*

Displacement is probably the weakest disadvantage here, at least where subsidies are targeted on the long-term unemployed. The subsidy aims to help the long-term unemployed become part of the effective supply of labour. If the long-term unemployed displace others, unemployment will still fall. The argument is exactly as already made in Chapter 7. Myth 2 was the idea that a larger labour force led to more unemployment. We hope we demolished this idea.

Remedy 3: Raising skills

The last policy that is part of 'from welfare to work', adult training, is another name for Remedy 3. The aim of adult training is to raise skills and so lower the unemployment that is due to insufficient demand for low-skilled workers. The companion volume *The UK Labour Market* looks at adult training. One reason for training adults in employment is to ensure that their skills remain in demand, which can reduce mismatch and so prevent unemployment. Here, however, we shall limit our discussion to training for the unemployed. As we saw in Chapter 4, the British experience of training the unemployed is not encouraging, and looking abroad may give pointers to more effective policies.

Sweden has an 'employment principle' which gives people unemployed for 300 days or more a **right to work or train**. The training is high-quality: the cost of each place is $2\frac{1}{2}$ times what is spent on Training for Work in this country. This makes extrainees attractive to employers. The right to work involves construction projects in the public sector, caring activities and subsidized private-sector employment. The Swedish 'employment principle' can be justified purely in terms of saving public spending if it brings about reduced

unemployment. In addition, those who advocate the adoption of a similar 'employment principle' here argue that the gain in human well-being and in output is substantial in relation to its costs. They also point to the massive backlog of housing maintenance and repairs and under-maintained hospitals and schools, the improvements that could be made to our environment and the growing need for community care. In terms of economics, it must promote efficiency, they argue, to bring together those needing work with the work that so desperately needs to be done.

Remedy 4: National economic assessment

A national economic assessment aims to create a national consensus on the level of pay increases that will enable the government to reduce unemployment without increasing inflation. The first stage in the national economic assessment is a variety of economic forecasts about the effect of different levels of pay increases. The government then invites employers and trade unions to discuss these forecasts before taking its decisions on taxes and spending. This is very much what already happens in Germany. In the UK a step towards a national economic assessment has already been taken with the Chancellor of the Exchequer's panel of independent forecasters, whose forecasts are published by the government. A national economic assessment is, it is claimed, very different from the incomes policies of the 1960s and 70s that we discussed in Chapter 4. It does not involve compulsion, but aims to encourage wage-setters, particularly employers, to take more account of the interests of the unemployed.

The UK has little experience of forming a national consensus on pay. Incomes policies tended to be imposed by governments. Still, policies for which there was a consensus did have some successes. Between October 1975 and October 1977, incomes policy brought annual wage inflation down from 29 per cent to 8 per cent, with little rise in unemployment. Without consensus in the early 1980s, a smaller reduction in inflation was only achieved at the expense of nearly 2 million people becoming unemployed, and many of them long-term unemployed. However, no-one now suggests repeating the incomes policy of the late 1970s. Most advocates of a national economic assessment acknowledge that incomes policies were too rigid to last. They imposed a limit on the pay increase of every group of employees. This was unacceptable to firms who use pay increases as a method of recruiting, retaining and motivating their labour force. It was also unacceptable to unions, for whom pay bargaining is a central function.

Remedy 5: Currency markets and interest rates

Targeting, 'from welfare to work', raising skills and a national economic assessment are all designed to permit lower unemployment without rising inflation. However, inflation could still rise as a result of increased demand. The reaction of **international currency markets** could sharply lower the value of the pound. *International currency markets involve the exchange of one currency for another – e.g. pounds for deutschmarks – and so determine how much each currency is worth in terms of other currencies.* A lower value of the pound means higher prices for imported goods, thus pushing up inflation.

This currency-market reaction is avoided in a fixed exchange rate system. However, the pound's experience in the European exchange rate mechanism was not a happy one (see Chapter 5). At least in the near future, it seems likely that the pound will float in the international currency markets. The government has two ways to maintain the value of the pound in a floating exchange rate system. First, it can buy pounds in exchange for foreign currency. This reduces our foreign exchange reserves, and does not always work (as was seen in September 1992). Second, the government can raise interest rates. This makes the pound more attractive in currency markets because people who keep their money in sterling now receive higher interest payments. Some then argue that raising interest rates can counter the effect of increased demand on the value of the pound. The problem

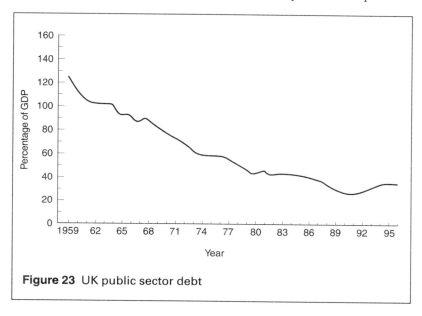

Figure 23 UK public sector debt

here is that higher interest rates reduce demand and so act directly against a policy of increased demand.

The suggested remedies for unemployment all increase government spending at least in the short term. The currency and money markets might react by pushing down the pound and creating pressure for higher interest rates. Such a reaction might be a matter of sentiment, rather than being justified in strict economic terms. Government borrowing (the **public sector borrowing requirement**) and the 'national debt' (that is **public sector debt**) are much lower than in many other countries. Figure 23 shows that, despite a recent increase, public sector debt is still much lower than in earlier years. (See the companion volume *UK Fiscal Policy* for more on these issues.) Still, the danger of a fall in the value of the pound and of a rise in interest rates is real and this is a powerful argument against the remedies. One suggestion for avoiding this problem is a **windfall tax** on formerly nationalized industries, such as the electricity, gas and water industries, to finance increased spending on active labour market policy. If government borrowing does not even increase in the short term, the value of the pound and the level of interest rates should not be affected.

KEY WORDS

Targeting	Deadweight costs
Long-term unemployment	Displacement
From welfare to work	Short-termism
Raising skills	Right to work or train
National economic assessment	International currency markets
National Insurance contributions	Public sector borrowing requirement
Job search measures	Public sector debt
Recruitment subsidies	Windfall tax
Adult training	

Reading list
National Institute of Economic and Social Research (NIESR), *The UK Economy*, Chapter 7, Heinemann Educational, 1995.

Essay topics
1. Which two objectives of macroeconomic policy do you consider to be the most important for the UK Government to pursue in the late 1990s? Justify your answer. [40 marks]

Explain how these objectives might conflict with each other and with other macroeconomic goals. [60 marks]
[University of London Examinations and Assessment Council 1996]

2. Keynes's solution to unemployment was higher public spending, which would add to incomes and, through the multiplier process, lead to more jobs. (*Economics Today*, September 1993)
   (a) Explain how Keynes's solution is supposed to work. [13 marks]
   (b) Are there any other solutions to the problem of unemployment? [12 marks]
   [University of Cambridge Local Examinations Syndicate 1996]

3. What is the economic rationale underlying a government 'spending its way out of recession'? [10 marks]
   To what extent is its ability to do so limited? [15 marks]
   [University of Oxford Delegacy of Local Examinations 1995]

4. Explain the basis for supply-side measures to cure unemployment. Discuss whether or not the principal measures taken by the Government to deal with unemployment in recent years have been successful. [25 marks]
   [Northern Examinations and Assessment Board 1995]

Data Response Question

Productivity, employment and earnings in the UK

This task is based on a question set by the University of London Examinations and Assessment Council in 1997. Study Figures A and B, read the article by Lloyds Bank and answer the questions.

1. Examine how the microeconomic factors, outlined in the passage, might have helped to make labour markets more efficient. [20 marks]

2. Explain how the macroeconomic environment has affected the UK labour market. [10 marks]

3. With reference to the passage, examine the possible reasons why high unemployment has neither improved price competitiveness nor reduced the growth of real earnings. [20 marks]

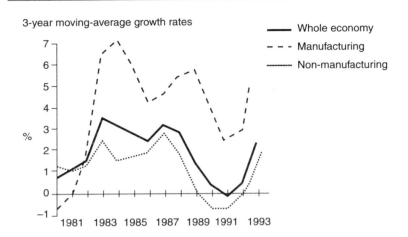

3-year moving-average growth rates

Whole economy
Manufacturing
Non-manufacturing

Figure A Productivity

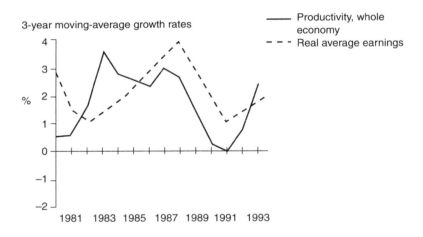

3-year moving-average growth rates

Productivity, whole economy
Real average earnings

Figure B Productivity and earnings growth

The last ten years have seen significant changes in UK government policy towards labour markets and in labour legislation, designed to make labour markets more efficient. Trade union power has been reduced, official intervention in wage setting (for instance on minimum wages) has declined, the tax and benefit system has been revised to improve work incentives, companies have been encouraged to link pay to performance (for instance through profit-related pay) and increased emphasis has been given to training.

Other factors have affected the working of labour markets in recent years. There is strong evidence of changes in industrial relations management in firms. The measures described above have coincided with, and perhaps encouraged, a shift towards much more decentralised pay setting in the 1980s. Within firms, there has been growing emphasis on pay setting at the business unit level, the obvious incentive being to link pay more closely to performance.

The macroeconomic environment has had important influences on the labour market. The last ten years have been a time of strong competitive pressures on UK industry, which have led to high levels of unemployment relative to previous decades.

There is some evidence that productivity growth in manufacturing has risen in the 1980s but the performance of non-manufacturing has been much less impressive, so that economy-wide productivity growth shows no improvement on earlier decades.

It appears that insofar as productivity growth has improved, this has been reflected in better pay for those in work, rather than in higher employment. Real earnings have followed productivity trends reasonably closely in the last ten years, with changes in productivity growth leading changes in real earnings growth by 1–2 years. Meanwhile, there have been greater fluctuations in employment, perhaps because it is less costly to hire and dismiss workers.

There has been little, if any, change in the relationship between earnings growth and unemployment. The rise in unemployment in the early 1990s appears to have had relatively little impact on the growth of real earnings. However, whilst the behaviour of overall earnings appears to have changed little in the 1980s, this hides significant changes in the distribution of earnings. One calculation suggests that the earnings of the highest paid 10% were 5.5 times those of the lowest paid 10% in 1989, compared with a ratio of 3.9 in 1979.

Insofar as our productivity performance has improved in the last decade, this has done nothing to improve our price competitiveness position relative to other countries because of the offsetting growth of earnings. Overall, the evidence would appear to suggest that the UK labour market retains too much inflexibility.

Source: 'Pay Versus Jobs in the 1990s', in *Lloyds Bank Economic Bulletin*, No. 175, July 1993

Conclusion

During the 'golden age of Keynesianism' that lasted for 20 years after the Second World War, unemployment, it was universally agreed, had been slain. The economic ideas of J M Keynes were widely believed to have provided a formula, demand management, for ending unemployment. In the 1960s and 1970s demand management led to higher inflation rather than lower unemployment. Economists had used the Phillips curve to describe a simple and stable trade-off between unemployment and inflation. The notion of the Phillips curve did not survive the 1970s, when unemployment and inflation rose at the same time. The Labour government accepted that demand management could not solve the problems of unemployment and inflation.

For the last 20 years, lower inflation has been a higher priority for UK governments than reduced unemployment. Indeed, unemployment is seen as a nasty but necessary side effect of the battle against inflation. Yet, even though inflation in the UK has been reduced to levels comparable to those of 20 or 30 years ago, unemployment shows no sign of disappearing of its own accord. Indeed, many commentators think that the current level of unemployment, which would have been unthinkable 20 years ago, is leading to inflationary pressures.

If unemployment is above the NAIRU, inflation falls, and if unemployment is below the NAIRU, inflation rises. So, trying to reduce employment without changing the NAIRU simply leads to increased inflation. The UK experience suggests that policies to reduce inflation increase unemployment. To obtain lower unemployment without increasing inflation, or lower inflation without increasing unemployment, requires measures which lower the NAIRU.

A companion volume of this book, *UK Current Economic Policy,* gives the three first aims of economic policy as: the fastest sustainable rate of growth in output; the lowest possible level of unemployment; low inflation.

Reducing the NAIRU allows lower unemployment and inflation at the same time. Lower unemployment means higher employment and so more output and faster growth, at least in the short term. Further, putting more of the labour force into work would improve the distribution of income and effective training policies increase productivity.

Unemployment remains a serious social problem. The number of households with adults of working age none of whom is working remains at record levels despite the recent fall in unemployment. The election of a new Labour government pledged to reduce unemployment by the use of many of the remedies discussed in Chapter 8 should provide a practical test of the idea that government has the power to reduce unemployment.

Index